GOOD
HOUSEKEEPING
**COOK AHEAD
RECIPES**

GOOD HOUSEKEEPING
COOK AHEAD RECIPES

BOOK CLUB ASSOCIATES

LONDON

This edition published 1975 by
Book Club Associates
by arrangement with
Ebury Press

Edited by Gill Edden

Colour pictures by
Stephen Baker, Anthony Blake, Michael Boys,
Barry Bullough, John Cook, Frank Coppins,
Gina Harris, and Michael Neale

Filmset by BAS Printers Limited, Wallop, Hampshire
and printed and bound in Italy by
Interlitho, S.p.a., Milan

Contents

Conversion to Metric Measurements

The recipes in this book were not converted by rule of thumb from imperial versions, but were tested and written up using metric weights and measures, based on a 25 g unit instead of the ounce (28.35 g). Slight adjustments to this basic conversion standard were necessary in some recipes to achieve satisfactory cooking results.

If you want to convert your own recipes from imperial to metric, we suggest you use the same 25 g unit, and use 500 ml in place of 1 pint, with the British Standard 5-ml and 15-ml spoons replacing the old variable teaspoons and tablespoons; these adaptations will, however, give a slightly smaller recipe quantity and may require a shorter cooking time.

For more exact conversions and general reference, the following tables will be helpful.

Metric Conversion Scale

CAPACITY	MASS	LENGTH
$\frac{1}{4}$ pint = 142 ml	1 oz = 28.35 g	1 in = 2.54 cm
$\frac{1}{2}$ pint = 284 ml	2 oz = 56.7 g	6 in = 15.2 cm
1 pint = 568 ml	4 oz = 113.4 g	100 cm = 1 metre
$\frac{1}{2}$ litre = 0.88 pints	8 oz = 226.8 g	= 39.37 in
1 litre = 1.76 pints	12 oz = 340.2 g	
	16 oz = 453.6 g	
	1 kilogram = 2.2 lb	

Note: ml = millilitre (s); cm = centimetre (s); g = gram (s)

Oven Temperature Scales

°CELSIUS SCALE	ELECTRIC SCALE °F	GAS OVEN MARKS
110°C	225°F	$\frac{1}{4}$
130	250	$\frac{1}{2}$
140	275	1
150	300	2
170	325	3
180	350	4
190	375	5
200	400	6
220	425	7
230	450	8
240	475	9

Foreword

Given the know-how, there's no limit to the number of dishes you can prepare and cook ahead of time. There are snags though if you don't know how long a dish will take to reheat and whether or not a night in the fridge will reduce a quiche to a sad, soggy mess. You'll find the answers here with enough recipes—all tested and tried by the Good Housekeeping Institute team of home economists—to take the worry out of cooking ahead for entertaining as well as family meals. Brenda Holroyd, a former member of GHI's staff, has chosen the recipes and has added mouth-watering menu suggestions for would be entertainers.

If you have any queries about recipes in this book do write to us at Good Housekeeping Institute, Chestergate House, Vauxhall Bridge Road, London SW1V 1HF.

Director
Good Housekeeping Institute

1. Dinner Dishes

It's fun to entertain, but not so funny if you have to spend most of the time in the kitchen, appearing only intermittently – and looking dishevelled – among your guests. These main dishes can be partly prepared beforehand – the day before, or early the same day, depending on when you have most time. Then they require only a few finishing touches, such as garnishing or thickening, in addition to reheating.

When you reheat casseroles and stews on top of the stove, bring them quickly to boiling point and then allow them to simmer for 15 minutes or for as long as necessary to heat through properly. Keeping meat warm, but not boiling, for long periods may encourage the growth of fresh bacteria.

You can also heat casseroles through in a moderate oven – allow about an hour for a 4–6 serving amount.

Sage-and-bacon stuffed pork

2½ lb. loin of pork (boned weight)
¼ lb. sweet-cure back bacon rashers, rinded
12 fresh or 6 dried sage leaves
oil
salt and pepper
flour
stock or vegetable water

SERVES 6

1 day ahead
Place the meat (ask your butcher to score the rind deeply and evenly) on a flat surface, fat side down. Cut the flesh to open it out a little. Lay the bacon rashers over the flesh and then place sage leaves at intervals. Roll up carefully and secure firmly with string, parcel fashion. Refrigerate.

When required
Place the joint in a roasting tin. Rub the rind thoroughly with oil and salt. Roast in the centre of the oven at 375°F, 190°C (mark 5) for 30–35 minutes per lb. stuffed weight plus 30 minutes. Remove the string, place the meat on a serving dish and return it to a low oven to keep warm.

Drain off all but 1 tbsp. fat. To make gravy,

stir in 2 level tsps. flour. Cook for a few minutes then gradually add about ½ pt. stock or vegetable water. Check seasoning and bring to the boil. Simmer for a few minutes.

Nasi goreng

4 oz. onion, skinned and
  chopped
1 clove garlic, skinned and
  crushed
2 oz. butter
8 oz. long grain rice
½ level tsp. coriander powder
½ level tsp. caraway seeds
½ level tsp. chili powder
1 level tsp. curry powder
1 tbsp. soy sauce
1 lb. cold roast pork, diced
½ lb. frozen peas
1 egg
2 tbsps. water
salt and pepper
tomato wedges

SERVES 4

1 day ahead
Fry the onion and garlic in the butter until soft but not coloured. Cook the rice in plenty of boiling salted water until cooked but still firm – about 12 minutes. Drain it and rinse under cold water. Stir the spices and soy sauce into the onion and cook for 1–2 minutes. Cool and store the onion and rice separately until required.

When required
Return the onion mixture to the pan and heat through, then stir in the meat and heat it thoroughly. Meanwhile cook the peas in salted water. Add the cooked rice to the meat mixture, blending all the ingredients. When the meat and rice are thoroughly heated, add the peas. Keep warm.

Break the egg into a bowl, whisk lightly and add 2 tbsps. water and seasoning.

At the last possible moment
Lightly grease the base of a frying pan and pour

Nasi goreng (*see above*)

Sage-and-bacon stuffed pork (*see page 9*)

in this omelette mixture. When it is set, turn it out on to a warm, greased baking sheet and cut into strips. Turn the nasi goreng into a serving dish and decorate the top with a lattice of omelette. Garnish with tomato wedges.

Pork chops in orange-pepper sauce

4 trimmed pork loin chops
salt and pepper
1 oz. sugar
1 oz. butter
1 clove garlic, skinned and
  sliced
1 oz. cornflour
½ level tsp. dried rosemary
½ pt. water
3 tbsps. lemon juice
3 tbsps. orange juice
½ green pepper, seeded and
  chopped
6 thick slices fresh orange

SERVES 4

1 day ahead
Season both sides of chops with salt, pepper, and a little sugar. Melt the butter in a frying pan and brown the chops well on both sides with the garlic. Place the chops on one side; discard the garlic. Add the rest of the sugar, cornflour and rosemary to the drippings. Stir well and gradually add the water then cook, stirring, until glossy. Add the juices and green pepper. Return the chops to the pan and place a slice of orange on top of each chop. Cover with a lid, plate, or foil, and simmer over a low heat for 40 minutes until the chops are tender, basting occasionally. Cool quickly and transfer carefully to a casserole. Refrigerate, covered.

45 minutes ahead
Reheat the casserole in the oven at 375°F, 190°C (mark 5) for 45 minutes, uncovering after 30 minutes. Meanwhile, halve 2 slices of fresh orange for garnish.

Pork with peas

3 tbsps. soy sauce
2 level tbsps. cornflour
½ level tsp. salt
1½ lb. pork fillet or tenderloin
1½ tbsps. corn oil
½ level tsp. sugar
¾ pt. chicken stock
¾ lb. frozen peas
For garnish
1½ oz. walnut halves
1 tbsp. corn oil

SERVES 6

1 day ahead
In a bowl, stir together the soy sauce, cornflour and salt. Cut the pork into fork-sized pieces. Heat the oil and fry the pork until evenly browned. Add the sugar and stock and mix well. Bring to the boil, stirring, cover, reduce the heat and simmer until the meat is tender – about 30 minutes. Cool, then refrigerate in a covered container.

30 minutes ahead
Put the mixture into a saucepan and add the peas. Bring to the boil and cook for 10 minutes. Meanwhile, fry the walnuts in oil until they colour. Scatter them over the pork before serving. Border the pork with boiled rice and serve with a tossed green salad.

Pork-stuffed peppers

4 large or 6 small green
   peppers
1 onion, skinned and finely
   chopped
1 oz. lard
2 oz. long grain rice
$\frac{3}{4}$ pt. beef stock, made from a
   cube
1 lb. pork ring (from a
   delicatessen)
2 tbsps. chopped parsley
salt and pepper
1 lb. tomatoes, skinned and
   seeded
1 level tbsp. flour
$\frac{1}{2}$ level tsp. sugar

SERVES 4

1 day ahead
Remove a thin slice from the stem end of each pepper, scoop out the seeds and membrane. Blanch the peppers and tops in boiling water for 2 minutes, cool and refrigerate.

Fry the onion in half the lard. Add the rice, stir and continue to cook gently until opaque. Stir in half the stock, cover and simmer for 12 minutes until the liquid is completely absorbed.

Skin and coarsely mince the pork ring. Stir it into the rice with the parsley and season the mixture well. If the mixture looks rather dry, add 1–2 tbsps. water. Cool and refrigerate it.

To make the sauce, fry the remaining onion in the remaining lard until soft but not coloured. Chop the tomatoes, add them to the onion and cook to a pulp. Sprinkle with flour, pour on the remaining stock, and simmer until thickened. Season well and stir in the sugar. Cool and refrigerate separately.

1 hour ahead
Stuff the peppers with the rice and pork and replace the lids. Put in an ovenproof dish. Pour the sauce over the peppers, cover and cook in the oven at 375°F, 190°C (mark 5) for about 30 minutes.

Note: Peppers, stuffing and sauce must be kept separately, covered, in a cool place until they are to be cooked.

Pork with wine sauce

8 prunes
salt and pepper
4 boneless pork chops
2 tbsps. oil
2 oranges
$\frac{1}{2}$ pt. water
12 tbsps. sherry or Madeira

SERVES 4

1 day ahead
Pour some boiling water over the prunes and simmer for 20 minutes or until tender. Pare the rind thinly from the oranges, completely free of white pith; cut it into very fine shreds, put these into a saucepan with $\frac{1}{2}$ pt. water and boil for 5 minutes. Add 4 tbsps. juice squeezed from the oranges and remove from the heat.

30 minutes ahead
Season the chops and fry slowly in the oil, allowing about 7 minutes on each side. Remove the chops from the frying pan and pour in the orange liquid; add the drained prunes and sherry or Madeira and

heat through. Keep warm. Serve the chops with the prunes and sauce poured over.

Piquant stuffed neck of lamb

1 oz. fresh white breadcrumbs
6 oz. pork sausage meat
2 oz. onion, skinned and finely chopped
salt and freshly ground black pepper
2 tbsps. stem ginger syrup
2 pieces (1 oz.) stem ginger
4 oz. pickled walnuts
2 lb. (boned weight) best-end of neck of lamb with breast flap attached
butter
parsley to garnish

SERVES 6

1 day ahead
Combine the breadcrumbs, sausage meat, onion and seasoning together. Pour the ginger syrup over. Finely chop the ginger and walnuts and work them evenly into the sausage meat. Wipe the lamb with a damp cloth. Trim off excess fat to give a neat shape and spread the filling over in an even layer. Roll up and secure at intervals with string. Note the weight of the joint, dot it with butter. Refrigerate.

About $1\frac{3}{4}$ hours ahead
Place the meat in a lightly greased roasting tin and cook in the oven at 350°F, 180°C (mark 4) for 40 minutes per lb. When cooked, slice the joint into six even slices. Remove the string and place these slices on a hot serving platter. Garnish with parsley. Skim the fat from the pan juices. Bring them to the boil and reduce to a rich glaze. Serve separately in a sauce-boat.

Arabian lamb

2 breasts of lamb, totalling $2\frac{1}{2}$ lb.
2 tbsps. oil
2 oz. long grain rice
$1\frac{1}{2}$ level tsps. salt
$\frac{1}{2}$ level tsp. pepper
2 cloves garlic, skinned and crushed
6 oz. onion, skinned and chopped
4 oz. green pepper, seeded and chopped
2 tbsps. chopped parsley
1 oz. pine kernels or nibbed almonds
$2\frac{1}{4}$-oz. can tomato paste

SERVES 4

The lamb should be butchered to leave the skin along one side, the bones cracked along the other side.

1 day ahead
Heat the oil in the frying pan. Stir in the rice and cook it until brown; add half the salt and pepper with the garlic, onion, green pepper and parsley. Cook, stirring, for 3–4 minutes then stir in the nuts and 8 fl. oz. water and bring to the boil. Cover and simmer for 10 minutes. Uncover, and cook until the water is absorbed. Cool.

To stuff the lamb, start at the flap end, pulling away the skin and fat layer from the meat to $\frac{1}{2}$ in. from the sides to make a pocket. Divide the filling between the pockets. Secure the opening with wooden cocktail sticks. Place the joint in a roasting tin, skin side up, sprinkle with the remaining seasonings and refrigerate.

3 hours ahead

Combine the tomato paste and 8 fl. oz. water. Pour it over the meat and bake uncovered in the oven at 350°F, 180°C (mark 4) for $2\frac{1}{2}$ hours, basting occasionally. 45 minutes before the end of the cooking time, place the casseroled yellow rice (which can be prepared and ready to cook, see recipe below) in the oven above the lamb.

Remove the cocktail sticks. Carve the meat into portions through the bone and arrange it over the rice. Glaze with the skimmed, boiled juices.

Serve with casseroled yellow rice, aubergine au gratin (see Salads and Vegetables chapter) and a salad of tomato, onion and cucumber.

Casseroled yellow rice
(for Arabian Lamb)

4 oz. dried apricots
8 oz. long grain rice
$\frac{1}{2}$ level tsp. salt
3 oz. onion, skinned and finely chopped
1 oz. seedless raisins
$\frac{1}{2}$ level tsp. ground turmeric

SERVES 4

1 day ahead

Scissor-snip the apricots into small dice. Place in a basin, pour over $1\frac{1}{4}$ pt. boiling water and leave to stand for 1 hour. Combine the rice, salt, onions, raisins and turmeric in an ovenproof casserole.

1 hour ahead

Re-boil the water and apricots and pour on to the contents of the casserole. Stir before covering and cook towards the top of the oven at 350°F, 180°C (mark 4) until the water is absorbed and the rice tender (about 1 hour).

Lamb oysters

6 lamb chump chops
1 oz. butter
$\frac{1}{2}$ small onion, skinned and grated
3 oz. mushrooms, wiped and chopped
1 tbsp. chopped parsley
grated rind of 1 lemon
1 egg yolk
salt and pepper
oil
2 tbsps. sherry

SERVES 6

1 day ahead

Trim the chops, discard the bones and cut pockets in the meat. Melt the butter, sauté the onion till soft and add the mushrooms. Off the heat, stir in the parsley, lemon rind and egg yolk. Season and when cool use this stuffing to fill the pockets; secure with wooden cocktail sticks. Refrigerate.

About 30 minutes ahead

Brush the frying pan with oil and brown the chops quickly on both sides. Lower the heat and cook for 15–20 minutes, turning once. Arrange the chops on a serving plate. Add the sherry to the pan juices, bubble, season and spoon it over the chops.

Lamb chops Cordon Bleu

4 4–5-oz. lamb chump chops
salt and freshly ground black
　　pepper
2 tbsps. oil
Dijon mustard
2 2–3-oz. slices cooked ham
1 egg, beaten
4 oz. fresh white breadcrumbs
1 clove garlic, skinned
1 oz. butter
4 thick slices Mozzarella
　　cheese
4 tomatoes, skinned and
　　halved
parsley

SERVES 4

1 day ahead
Trim the chops and discard the eye-bones. Mould the meat into neat shapes and secure if necessary with wooden cocktail sticks. Season both sides. Heat the oil and fry the chops slowly until tender – about 20 minutes. Drain the chops and keep the pan juices. Slice horizontally through the chops to make pockets. Spread each cut surface with mustard, and close. Divide each slice of ham in half and spread with more mustard. Press the ham mustard side against the chops then coat chops and ham evenly with beaten egg and press crumbs well in to cover the surface completely. Chill overnight in a covered dish.

30 minutes ahead
Rub a large frying pan with a cut clove of garlic. Heat together the reserved juices and the butter.
　　Remove the cocktail sticks and place the chops ham side down in hot fat and fry until golden. Turn, reduce the heat, and cook for about 10 minutes.

Just before serving
Arrange the chops, ham side up, in an ovenproof dish. Place cheese on top and grill to melt the cheese. Serve at once, garnished with grilled tomatoes and parsley.

Veal fricassee

1–1½ lb. stewing veal
½ lb. back bacon, cut in 2 thick
　　rashers
1 oz. butter
1 tbsp. oil
½ small onion, skinned and
　　finely chopped
½ pt. veal stock or water
salt and pepper
beurre manié (kneaded
　　butter – ¾ oz. flour worked
　　into ¾ oz. softened butter)
1–2 tbsps. lemon juice
2 slices white bread
parsley, for garnish

SERVES 4

1 day ahead
Cut the veal into even 1-in. cubes. Rind and trim the bacon and cut as for the veal. Melt the butter, add the oil and fry the veal and bacon until pale brown. Remove the meat and place it in a large casserole. Add the onion to the fat, fry and add to the casserole. Pour over the stock or water. Season and cover. Cook in the oven at 325°F, 170°C (mark 3) for 1½ hours. Cool and refrigerate, covered.

1 hour ahead
Reheat the fricassee on top of the stove in a sauce-pan, stirring gently. Strain off the liquor into a small pan and return the meat to the casserole. Drop small pieces of the beurre manié into the warm liquor; stir well to thicken, bring to the

boil and boil for 2–3 minutes. Add lemon juice and adjust the seasoning. Pour the sauce over the veal. Put the veal to reheat in the oven at 350°F, 180°C (mark 4) for about 1 hour, adjusting the sauce consistency if necessary. Meanwhile, toast the bread slices, cut them into triangles and use to garnish the veal, with the parsley. Serve with duchesse potatoes and baked tomatoes, which can be cooked in the oven while the veal is reheating.

Swiss veal

4 lb. pie veal, cubed
seasoned flour
2 tbsps. cooking oil
8 oz. carrots, peeled and diced
8 oz. shallots, skinned and
   chopped
1 tbsp. lemon juice
$\frac{1}{2}$ pt. stock
$\frac{3}{4}$ pt. dry white wine
bouquet garni
4 egg yolks, beaten
$\frac{1}{2}$ pt. natural yoghurt
salt and pepper
parsley, chopped

SERVES 8

1 day ahead
Dust the veal lightly with the seasoned flour. Heat the oil and fry the veal until pale golden. Add the carrots, shallots, lemon juice, stock, wine and bouquet garni and simmer gently until the meat is tender – about $1\frac{1}{4}$ hours. (Alternatively, turn the mixture into a casserole and cook at 350°F, 180°C (mark 4) for about $1\frac{1}{2}$ hours.) Cool and refrigerate, covered.

About 15 minutes ahead
Heat the meat mixture in a pan until bubbling. Blend the egg yolks with the yoghurt; add a little of the hot stock, then stir it into the mixture. Adjust seasoning and reheat gently without boiling; serve sprinkled with chopped parsley. Serve with new potatoes and green beans.

Veal and rice paprika

1 oz. butter
1 lb. pie veal, cut into small
   pieces
6 oz. onion, skinned and finely
   sliced
1 level tsp. paprika
1 level tbsp. tomato paste
$\frac{3}{4}$ pt. stock
6 oz. long grain rice
$\frac{1}{4}$ pt. soured cream
salt and pepper
chopped parsley for garnish

SERVES 4

1 day ahead
Melt the butter in a frying pan. When it is on the point of turning brown, add the veal and fry briskly. Transfer the meat to a casserole and fry the onion until tender. Stir in the paprika, tomato paste and stock. Pour over the veal, cover and cook in the oven at 325°F, 170°C (mark 3) for about 1 hour, or until tender. Cool and refrigerate, covered.

1 hour ahead
Reheat the casserole in the oven at 325°F, 170°C (mark 3) for about 20 minutes, then add the rice, cover and return it to the oven for a further 30 minutes. Gently heat the soured cream in a small pan and fork it through the rice. Season, and sprinkle with chopped parsley.

Veal and rice paprika (*see page 17*)

Beef pies

3½ lb. stewing steak
2 tbsps. red wine vinegar
10-fl.-oz. bottle pale ale
1 clove garlic, optional
2 tbsps. oil
6 oz. onion, skinned and
  sliced
4 level tbsps. flour
5-oz. can tomato paste
salt and freshly ground black
  pepper
13-oz. pkt. frozen puff pastry
beaten egg
paprika pepper
parsley to garnish

SERVES 6

2 days ahead
Trim the meat and cut it into 1–1½-in. pieces.
Marinade it in vinegar, ale and crushed garlic
overnight.

1 day ahead
Heat the oil and fry the onions until transparent.
Drain the meat and reserve the marinade. Dredge
the meat with flour and fry in the reheated oil to
seal the surfaces. Add the onions, tomato paste
and seasoning. Pour the marinade over. Bring to
the boil, stir and cook for 2–3 minutes. Turn
into a casserole and cook in the oven at 300°F,
150°C (mark 2) for about 2 hours. Cool and
refrigerate, covered.

About 2 hours ahead
Put pastry to thaw.

About 1 hour ahead
Roll out the pastry to a rectangle 14 in. by 18 in.
and cut it in half widthways. Brush with egg,
sprinkle with paprika and roll up from the long
side. Cut at an angle into ¼-in. slices. Divide the

Veal fricassee (*see page 16*)

meat between $6\frac{3}{4}$–1-pt. ovenproof dishes. Spoon over 1–2 tbsps. of the juices and arrange the pastry slices around the edge, overlapping. Brush with egg. Bake just above the oven centre at 400°F, 200°C (mark 6) for about 30 minutes. Garnish with parsley. Reheat the remaining meat juices to serve separately.

Burgundy beef

2 lb. topside of beef
1 oz. lard
4 oz. thick rashers streaky
   bacon, rinded
1 level tbsp. flour
$\frac{1}{4}$ pt. red Burgundy
$\frac{1}{4}$ pt. stock
pinch dried thyme
$\frac{1}{2}$ bayleaf
1 clove garlic, skinned and
   crushed
salt and pepper
$\frac{1}{2}$ oz. lard
6–12 shallots, skinned

SERVES 6

1 day ahead
Trim the meat and cut it into large cubes. Melt 1 oz. lard in a frying pan. Brown the meat on all sides, a few pieces at a time then place it in a $3\frac{1}{2}$-pt. casserole. Dice the bacon, add it to the frying pan and fry until beginning to colour. Stir in the flour and continue to cook until brown, stirring occasionally. Gradually stir in the wine and stock and bring to the boil. Add the thyme, bayleaf, crushed garlic and seasoning to taste. Pour over the meat. Cover, and cook in the oven at 325°F, 170°C (mark 3) for about $2\frac{1}{2}$ hours. Cool quickly and refrigerate, covered.

1 hour ahead
Melt $\frac{1}{2}$ oz. lard in a small pan and brown the shallots. Drain, add to the casserole and reheat in the oven at 350°F, 180°C (mark 4) for about 1 hour. Discard the bayleaf before serving.

Note: The shallots may also be browned a day ahead and added to the casserole before refrigeration.

Beef and pepper casserole

2 lb. chuck steak
1 oz. fat or oil
2 large onions, skinned and
   sliced
2 green peppers, seeded and
   sliced
$1\frac{1}{2}$ oz. flour
$1\frac{1}{2}$ pt. brown stock
2 level tbsps. tomato paste
salt and freshly ground black
   pepper
bouquet garni

SERVES 6

1 day ahead
Cut the meat into 1-in. cubes. Heat the fat or oil and fry the onions until golden brown; remove and place them in a casserole. Reserve a few slices of pepper and fry the rest lightly. Add these to the onions in the casserole. Brown the meat in the remaining fat, adding only a few pieces at a time so that the fat remains really hot. When the meat is well browned, transfer it to the casserole with the vegetables. Add the flour to the fat remaining in the frying pan, stir well and gradually stir in the stock and tomato paste. Bring to the boil, season and pour over the meat and vegetables in the casserole. Add the bouquet garni.

Cover and cook in the centre of the oven at 350°F, 180°C (mark 4) for 1–1½ hours. Cool and refrigerate, covered.

30 minutes ahead
Reheat in the oven at 400°F, 200°C (mark 6), adding the reserved slices of pepper after 10 minutes. Remove the bouquet garni before serving.

Serve with a green salad and crusty bread and butter. For 6 people you will need 1 large lettuce, 1 bunch of watercress, 1 head of chicory and 1 green pepper. Wash and trim, slicing the chicory and pepper. The salad can be prepared early in the day and stored in the refrigerator – but not mixed. Just before serving, toss in French dressing.

Beef olives

8 slices beef topside, cut about
    ¼ in. thick and 2½ in. by 3 in.
¼ lb. button mushrooms
1 large tomato, skinned and
    seeded
1 small onion, skinned and
    quartered
2 oz. fresh white breadcrumbs
2 tbsps. chopped parsley
1 level tsp. chopped mixed
    fresh herbs
1 oz. suet, shredded
salt and pepper
1 egg yolk
dripping, for frying
¾ pt. stock or tomato juice
butter, for frying
1 level tbsp. flour
parsley, to garnish

SERVES 4

1 day ahead
Remove all the fat from the beef. Wipe and peel the mushrooms and trim the stalks level with the caps. Chop the tomato finely. Mince the fat with the mushroom skins and stalks and the onion. Add the breadcrumbs, herbs, suet and tomato; mix well, season and bind with the egg yolk.

Flatten each piece of beef by beating with a rolling pin or a meat bat. Divide the stuffing into 8, and place a portion in the centre of each piece of steak. Roll up carefully and secure with fine string or wooden cocktail sticks. Brown the olives in a little melted dripping, then arrange in a casserole. Pour over the hot stock or tomato juice and cook in the oven at 325°F, 170°C (mark 3) for about 2 hours until tender. Cool quickly and refrigerate.

1 hour ahead
Reheat in the oven at 325°F, 170°C (mark 3) for 45 minutes, turning the olives after 20 minutes. Sauté the mushrooms in a little butter and keep them warm. Strain off the gravy and thicken it with the flour.

Remove the string from the olives; dish them up and garnish with mushrooms and parsley. Serve with buttered rice and a green salad.

Note: Boil and drain the rice the day before; cool and cover and store it in the refrigerator. Just before required, toss in melted butter until hot.

Beef and chestnut casserole

3–3½ lb. chuck steak
2 oz. seasoned flour
2 oz. lard
1 medium onion, skinned and
    sliced
15-oz. can peeled tomatoes
4-oz. can pimientos, drained
    and sliced
¼ pt. hot water
1 beef stock cube
¼ pt. red wine
salt and pepper
3 oz. sliced garlic sausage
12 whole canned chestnuts,
    drained
melted butter
parsley for garnish

SERVES 6

1 day ahead
Trim the fat from the steak. Cut the meat into 2-in. pieces and toss in seasoned flour; retain the excess flour. Melt the lard in a frying pan and fry the meat, browning a few pieces at a time. Place the meat, when ready, in a large casserole. Add the onion to the pan and fry gently until beginning to brown. Stir in the excess flour then gradually add the tomatoes and pimientos.

Blend the water and stock cube and add with the wine to the frying pan. Bring to the boil and check seasoning. Cut the garlic sausage into strips. Add it to the beef in the casserole and pour the stock and wine over. Cover the casserole and cook in the oven at 325°F, 170°C (mark 3) for about 3 hours. Cool and refrigerate, covered.

1 hour ahead
Place the casserole in the oven at 350°F, 180°C

Beef and pepper casserole (*see page 20*)

22

Beef and chestnut casserole (*see above*)

(mark 4) for about 1 hour. Transfer to a clean hot casserole for serving. Sauté 12 drained chestnuts in a little melted butter until browned. Add to the casserole. Garnish with parsley.

Burgundy beef galantine

3 lb. chuck steak (in 1 piece)
$\frac{3}{4}$ lb. back bacon rashers, rinded
salt and pepper
2 oz. butter
1 tbsp. cooking oil
1 large onion, skinned and sliced
1 large carrot, peeled and sliced
1 bayleaf
1 level tsp. dried herbs
$\frac{1}{2}$ pt. red wine – preferably Burgundy
$\frac{1}{2}$ pt. water
$\frac{1}{2}$ lb. button mushrooms, wiped and sliced
$\frac{1}{2}$ oz. powdered gelatine

SERVES 6

1 day ahead
Trim all the excess fat from the meat and discard. Lay the bacon rashers over the meat to cover it completely and tie into a long roll with string. Sprinkle the roll with salt and pepper. Heat 1 oz. butter and the oil in a large flameproof casserole. Add the meat and fry, turning it until sealed all over. Add the onion, carrot, herbs, wine and $\frac{1}{2}$ pt. water. Bring to the boil, cover, and cook in the oven at 350°F, 180°C (mark 4) for 3 hours.

Remove the meat from the pan and leave it until quite cold. Place the stock in the refrigerator; when it is cold, skim off the fat and discard. Make the stock up to 1 pt. with water, if necessary. Melt the remaining butter in a frying pan and sauté the mushrooms; leave until cold. Cut the meat into thin slices; arrange half of these in a 3–4-pt. loaf tin, cover with the mushrooms, then the remaining sliced meat. Dissolve the gelatine in 2 tbsps. water in a basin held over a pan of hot water; add to the stock and mix well. Leave it to stand and, when beginning to set, pour it over the meat and mushrooms. Leave in refrigerator until completely set.

When required
Unmould and slice for serving. Serve with tomato and watercress salad and French bread and butter.

Beef Eldorado

2 small onions, skinned
4 young carrots, scraped
3 tbsps. cooking oil
1 lb. lean chuck steak, cubed
seasoned flour
$\frac{1}{2}$ pt. light ale
$\frac{1}{4}$ level tbsp. black treacle
3 oz. sultanas
salt and pepper

SERVES 4

1 day ahead
Thickly slice the onions; cut the carrots into thin rings. Heat the oil and fry the onions and carrots for about 2 minutes; remove from the pan. Toss the meat in seasoned flour and fry it until lightly coloured. Return the vegetables to the pan, pour in the light ale, bring to the boil and add the treacle and sultanas. Place in an ovenproof dish, cover, and cook in the oven at 325°F, 170°C (mark 3) for $1\frac{1}{2}$ hours. Check seasoning. Cool quickly and refrigerate, covered.

1 hour ahead
Remove the lid and cover loosely with foil. Reheat in the oven at 350°F, 180°C (mark 4) for about 1 hour, until bubbling. Serve accompanied by natural yoghurt sprinkled with chopped parsley.

Smyrna sausages

2 small slices white bread
milk
1 lb. lean minced beef
2 small onions, skinned and
    minced
a little chopped parsley and
    mint
$\frac{1}{4}$ level tsp. powdered cumin or
    mixed spice
1 egg, beaten
3–4 tbsps. oil or melted butter
3–4 level tbsps. plain flour
10 level tbsps. tomato paste
1 level tsp. sugar
8 fl. oz. dry white wine
8 fl. oz. water
salt and pepper

SERVES 4

1 day ahead
Remove the crusts from the bread, soak the soft part in a little milk and squeeze it almost dry. Place the meat in a basin with half the minced onion, the soaked bread, chopped parsley, mint and the spice. Bind the mixture with beaten egg and knead well. Shape the mixture into small sausages about 2 in. long. Refrigerate in a covered container.

Prepare the tomato sauce. Fry the remaining minced onion in butter until soft but not coloured; add the flour, tomato paste, sugar, wine, water, salt and pepper and simmer for a few minutes. Store, when cool, in a covered basin in the refrigerator.

About 1 hour ahead
Fry the sausages in a little oil or butter until brown on all sides. Place carefully in a saucepan. Pour the sauce on to the sausages and simmer for 30–45 minutes, until the meat is cooked. Serve hot.

Flank of beef with horseradish

$2\frac{1}{2}$ lb. thick flank of beef (in
    1 piece)
$2\frac{1}{2}$ oz. butter
6 oz. onion, skinned and
    chopped
4 oz. fresh white breadcrumbs
4 oz. Cheddar cheese, finely
    chopped
3 level tbsps. horseradish
    relish
salt and freshly ground black
    pepper
1 egg, beaten
$\frac{1}{4}$ pt. water

SERVES 6

1 day ahead
Slice the meat almost through and open it out like a book. Lay the meat on a chopping board and beat well to flatten to an even thickness. Carefully score a diamond pattern on the newly cut surface of the meat.

Melt $1\frac{1}{2}$ oz. butter in a saucepan and sauté the onion. Off the heat, stir in the breadcrumbs and cheese. Stir in the horseradish relish and season with salt and pepper. Bind together with beaten egg. Place the stuffing down the length of the meat on the unscored side. Roll up and secure the meat with string. Refrigerate until required.

2 hours ahead
Place the meat on a large piece of foil in a baking tin. Pull up the sides of the foil to make a shallow container. Sprinkle the meat with black pepper,

dot with the remaining butter and pour in the water. Cook uncovered in the oven at 350°F, 180°C (mark 4) for $1\frac{3}{4}$ hours or until tender. Use the strained juices to make a thin gravy.

Serve with pan-sauté potatoes with chives (see Salads and Vegetables section) and mange-tout (sugar peas), cooked in boiling salted water for 5 minutes and then drained well.

Glazed baked salmon garni

$1\frac{1}{2}$-lb. piece middle cut fresh
 salmon
butter
$\frac{1}{2}$ pt. aspic jelly, made from
 aspic jelly powder
black olives, for garnish
cucumber slices, for garnish
12 very small tomatoes,
 skinned
$\frac{1}{2}$ lb. French beans, cooked and
 cooled
16-oz. can asparagus tips,
 drained
$\frac{1}{4}$ pt. French dressing

SERVES 4

1 day ahead
Generously butter a large piece of foil. Lay the prepared fish in the centre; join the edges carefully together to form a loose package. Place on a baking sheet and bake in the oven at 300°F, 150°C (mark 2) for about 1 hour. When the fish is cooked it should show signs of coming away from the bone. Unwrap the fish while still warm and remove the skin. Leave to cool. When it is completely cold, coat with a thin layer of aspic jelly.

About 1 hour ahead
Decorate with halved olives and cucumber slices. Place on a serving dish and garnish with a little chopped aspic. Surround with the tomatoes, beans and asparagus tips and spoon a little French dressing over the vegetables.

Chicken Beaujolais

4 rashers back bacon, rinded
 and cut up
cooking oil
4 chicken portions, skinned
2 oz. onion, skinned and finely
 sliced
$\frac{3}{4}$ oz. plain flour
$\frac{1}{4}$ pt. Beaujolais
$\frac{1}{4}$ pt. water
1 chicken stock cube
salt and pepper
4 tomatoes, skinned and
 quartered
chopped parsley, to garnish

SERVES 4

1 day ahead
Use a shallow, flameproof casserole large enough to take the chicken in a single layer. Without any extra fat, gently fry the bacon snippets until beginning to brown. Drain from the fat. Add just enough oil to the casserole to cover the base. Brown the chicken evenly and lightly, remove from the casserole and strain off all but 1 tbsp. fat. Add the onion and when it begins to colour, stir in the flour and cook for 1–2 minutes. With the casserole still over the heat, slowly stir in the wine, water and crumbled stock cube. Loosen the residue from the pan base and bring to the boil, stirring. Adjust the seasoning; replace the bacon and chicken, flesh side down; cover and cook for about $1\frac{1}{4}$ hours. Cool and refrigerate.

Glazed baked salmon garni (*see opposite*)

About 1 hour ahead
Tuck the tomato quarters into the corners in the casserole, cover, and reheat in the oven at 350°F, 180°C (mark 4) for about 45 minutes. Dish up the chicken with the sauce spooned over and garnished with chopped parsley. Serve with a green salad and French bread.

Lemon chicken double-crust pie

3-lb. oven-ready chicken
1½ oz. butter
3 level tbsps. flour
1–2 oz. grated cheese
2 level tbsps. chopped parsley
grated rind and juice of 1
   lemon
salt and freshly ground black
   pepper
12 oz. shortcrust pastry (12 oz.
   flour, etc.)
beaten egg or milk to glaze
8-oz. pkt. frozen asparagus
   spears

SERVES 6

1 day ahead
Remove the chicken giblets and cook the bird in a roaster bag with the oven at 375°F, 190°C (mark 5) for about 1½ hours. Drain off the chicken juices and make up to ½ pt. with water. Skin the chicken, strip the meat from the bird and chop it roughly. (The skin and carcass will form the basis of a good stock). Cool and refrigerate, covered.

Early on the day it is to be eaten
Melt 1 oz. butter in a pan, stir in the flour and cook for 1–2 minutes. Blend in the chicken juices to make a sauce; simmer a few minutes and stir in the cheese, chicken, parsley, lemon rind and 2–3 tbsps. lemon juice. Adjust seasoning and allow to cool.

1 hour ahead
Line a 10-in. metal or foil pie-plate with half the rolled pastry. Spread the filling over, damp the edges and top with a pastry lid. Seal the edges. Make a slit in the centre and brush with egg or milk. Bake at 400°F, 200°C (mark 6) for about 45 minutes. To serve, garnish with freshly cooked asparagus glazed with melted butter.

Cold ham soufflé

1 oz. butter
1 oz. plain flour
½ pt. milk
4 large eggs, separated
4 level tsps. powdered
   gelatine
4 tbsps. water
8 oz. cooked ham, finely
   minced
½ level tsp. chopped fresh
   tarragon (¼ level tsp. dried)
¼ pt. single cream
salt and pepper
cress and slices of ham for
   garnish

SERVES 4

In the morning (for the evening)
Prepare a 1-pt. capacity soufflé dish by tying a double band of greaseproof or non-stick paper round the outside, to stand about 3 in. above the rim of the dish. Melt the butter in a pan, stir in the flour and cook over a gentle heat for 2 minutes. Add the milk and bring to the boil, stirring constantly until the sauce thickens. Remove from the heat and beat in the egg yolks one at a time. Dissolve the gelatine in the water in a basin over a pan of hot water; add it to the sauce and leave in a cool place, stirring occasionally until it begins to set. Stir in the minced ham, tarragon and cream. Adjust seasoning according to taste; don't add too much salt – the ham may already be salty.

   Whisk the egg whites until stiff. Fold these into the ham mixture, turn it into the prepared soufflé dish and leave to set in the refrigerator.

1 hour before serving

Remove the soufflé from the refrigerator. Roll the ham slices and place a little cress in each end; wrap the rolls in plastic film till required. To serve, remove the string and paper collar; wet a palette knife under the hot tap and run it carefully between the double paper and the edge of the soufflé, gently peeling the paper away. Unwrap the ham rolls and use them to garnish the soufflé together with any remaining cress.

Cod basque

1 red pepper, seeded
4 tomatoes, skinned
1 level tsp. caster sugar
1 level tsp. tomato paste
1 level tsp. paprika pepper
1 clove garlic, skinned and
    crushed
1 tbsp. red wine vinegar
2 tbsps. corn oil
salt and freshly ground black
    pepper
4 frozen cod steaks

SERVES 4

Early on the day

Finely slice the pepper and blanch it in boiling water for 2 minutes. Drain. Slice the tomatoes. Combine the sugar, tomato paste, paprika, crushed garlic, vinegar, oil, pepper and seasoning.

About 45 minutes ahead

Place the cod steaks in a single layer in the base of buttered shallow ovenproof dish. Layer the sliced tomato and pepper mixture on top. Cover with foil and bake in the oven at 425°F, 220°C (mark 7) for about 30 minutes.

Roast duckling with grapefruit sauce

2 3½-lb. ducklings, thawed if
    frozen
salt and freshly ground black
    pepper
2 grapefruit
6¼-fl.-oz. can frozen con-
    centrated unsweetened
    grapefruit juice
1 level tbsp. arrowroot
water
2 level tbsps. plain flour

SERVES 6

Early on the day

Joint each duckling into six. Trim off the excess fat. Wipe and prick the flesh well and season it. Remove all peel and pith from the grapefruit and cut the flesh into segments. Cover and refrigerate the segments. Make the frozen fruit juice up to ¾ pt. with water, blend a little with the arrowroot in a small pan, add all the juice and bring to the boil, stirring. Leave, covered, in a cool place.

1½ hours ahead

Place the ducklings on a wire rack in a roasting tin. Cook near the top of the oven at 350°F, 180°C (mark 4) for 1¼–1½ hours. Baste with the pan juices twice during cooking. Twenty minutes before the end of cooking time sprinkle with flour and baste again. Transfer the cooked duckling portions to a preheated serving dish and arrange the fruit segments on top. Return them to the oven for a few minutes. Drain the fat from the roasting tin, leaving the duckling juices. Add the grapefruit sauce and heat thoroughly. Strain the sauce and use some to glaze the duckling. Serve the rest separately.

Dolmades

1 can vine leaves (or fresh
   cabbage leaves)
3 tbsps. lard or cooking oil
1 lb. cooked lean meat,
   minced
1–2 onions, skinned and sliced
2 tbsps. long grain rice
chopped parsley
a little tomato sauce
salt and pepper
juice of 1 lemon

SERVES 4

1 day ahead
Dip the leaves in boiling water for 1–2 minutes and leave to drain while the stuffing is prepared. Put 2 tbsps. lard or oil in a frying pan with the meat, onions, rice, parsley, tomato sauce and seasoning; mix well and fry, stirring, until the onions are transparent and meat is cooked. Cool. Add the lemon juice and put a small portion in the centre of each vine leaf; roll up and secure with fine string or skewers. Refrigerate.

20 minutes ahead
Put the dolmades in a pan with the remaining fat or oil, a little more tomato sauce and a little water. Cook over a low heat until the sauce is well reduced. Serve with boiled rice.

Cold ham soufflé (*see page 28*)

Dolmades (*see above*)

2. Serve with a Salad

Quiches and other pastry-based savoury dishes simplify cooking ahead; the pastry, fillings, and the salads that go with them can be largely prepared well in advance of the meal (see Chapter 5). Or the complete quiche can be made beforehand and heated through when required.

Cold meat dishes – including pies, loaves and moulds – are also delicious timesavers.

Quiche Lorraine

6 oz. shortcrust pastry (6 oz. flour, etc.)

For the filling
6 bacon rashers, rinded and chopped
2 medium sized onions, skinned and chopped
1 oz. butter
2 oz. Gruyère cheese, thinly sliced
4 tbsps. milk
4 tbsps. single cream
2 large eggs
salt and pepper

SERVES 4

1 day ahead
Put an 8-in. flan ring on a baking sheet (or use an 8-in. flan case) and line it with the prepared pastry. Leave it in the refrigerator to rest while you prepare the filling. Fry the bacon and onion in the melted butter for a few minutes, till the onion is transparent and the bacon cooking through; allow to cool. Place the thinly sliced cheese in the base of the pastry-lined flan ring. Spoon the onion and bacon mixture over. Make a custard by whisking the milk, cream, eggs and seasoning together and pour it over the filling in the flan case.

Bake at 400°F, 200°C (mark 6) until the pastry is crisp and the filling set. Remove from the oven and cool. Keep in the refrigerator.

30 minutes ahead
Refresh in the oven at 350°F, 180°C (mark 4) for 20 minutes. Serve warm, garnished with chopped parsley.

Alternative fillings
Prawn and spring onion
Fry ½ a bunch of washed, trimmed and chopped spring onions in 2 oz. butter for a few minutes, then stir in 4–6 oz. peeled prawns. Cool, place over the base of the flan case and cover with the custard mixture.

Bacon and sweetcorn

Trim and finely chop 6 rashers of bacon and fry in 2 oz. butter until just cooked. Drain a 7-oz. can of sweetcorn kernels, add to the pan and stir for 1 minute. Cool, place over the base of the flan case and cover with the custard mixture.

Haddock cheese

Cook an 8-oz. packet of boil-in-the-bag frozen haddock as directed. Remove it from the bag and discard the skin and any bones; flake with a fork and cool. Finely slice 2 oz. Gruyère cheese, use it to cover the base of the flan case, then top with the fish and the usual custard mixture.

Vitello tonnato

1½ lb. boned leg of veal
1 small carrot, peeled and
  quartered
1 small onion, skinned and
  quartered
1 stick of celery, scrubbed and
  chopped
4 peppercorns
1 level tsp. salt
2 oz. tuna in oil
4 anchovy fillets
¼ pt. olive oil (approx.)
2 egg yolks
pepper
1 tbsp. lemon juice
capers, gherkins, chopped
  parsley, tomato and lemon
  slices, for garnish

SERVES 4

1 day ahead

Tie the boned meat into a neat roll. Put the meat in a saucepan, with the bone if possible, the vegetables, peppercorns, salt and water just to cover. Bring to the boil, cover and simmer until tender – about 1 hour. Remove the meat and cool. Meanwhile, mash together the tuna, anchovy fillets and 1 tbsp. oil, using a wooden spoon; stir in the egg yolks and pepper. Press the mixture through a sieve into a small basin; add the lemon juice. Stir in the oil little by little, beating thoroughly after each addition, until the sauce has the consistency of thin cream. Slice the meat, arrange it in a shallow dish and coat completely with sauce. Cover closely and leave to marinade overnight in the refrigerator.

1 hour ahead

Remove from the refrigerator and garnish. Serve alone or with potato and beetroot salad.

Cold glazed bacon

4-lb. piece of collar or corner
  bacon
1 tbsp. clear honey
2 tbsps. white vinegar
Demerara sugar

SERVES 4–6

1 day ahead

Soak the bacon joint, which should be well strung, for 2 hours in cold water. Drain and place it skin side down in a large pan and cover with fresh cold water. Bring slowly to the boil; remove any scum. Reduce the heat and simmer uncovered for 20 minutes per lb. plus 20 minutes over. Always keep the joint under water (top up with fresh boiling water if necessary). Half an hour before the end of the cooking time, drain the joint, strip off the rind and, with a sharp knife, score the fat in a lattice pattern. Heat the honey and vinegar to combine them, brush the glaze over the joint and dredge with sugar, patting it well in. Crisp off in the oven, set at 350°F, 180°C (mark 4) until golden; baste with any excess honey glaze. Leave until cold, then wrap in foil and refrigerate.

1 hour ahead
Remove the joint from the refrigerator and allow to come to room temperature before serving.

Quiches simplify cooking ahead

Vitello tonnato (*see page 33*)

Lasagne

2 14-oz. cans tomatoes,
  drained
1 level tbsp. tomato paste
1 level tsp. dried marjoram
salt and freshly ground black
  pepper
1 lb. lean minced beef
4 oz. lasagne strips
1 oz. butter
1 oz. flour
$\frac{1}{2}$ pt. milk
6 oz. Cheddar cheese, grated
oil for glazing
4 oz. Mozzarella or Bel Paese
  cheese, sliced

SERVES 4

1 day ahead

Combine the canned tomatoes, tomato paste, marjoram, salt and pepper. Simmer in an open pan for 30 minutes. Add the mince and simmer for a further 25 minutes, still uncovered. Cook the lasagne strips in a large pan of fast boiling, salted water for 10–15 minutes and drain.

In a small saucepan, melt 1 oz. butter; stir in the flour and gradually blend in the milk. Bring to the boil, stirring constantly. Remove from the heat; add the Cheddar cheese and season.

Cover the base of an ovenproof dish (about $1\frac{1}{2}$ in. deep) with strips of lasagne. Add alternate layers of meat and cheese sauce. Finish the final layer with strips of pasta placed diagonally across, with the sauces spooned between. Lightly oil the pasta to prevent it drying. Cover and refrigerate.

1 hour ahead

Bake the lasagne in the oven at 375°F, 190°C (mark 5), uncovered, for about 45 minutes. Remove it from the oven and put the slices of Mozzarella on top of the cheese sauce. Raise the oven temperature to 425°F, 220°C (mark 7) and return the lasagne to the oven until the cheese is golden and bubbling. Serve immediately with dressed green salad.

Cannelloni au gratin

10 oz. cannelloni
a chunk of bread the size of an
    orange, without crust
milk
1 egg, hard-boiled and finely
    chopped
1 tbsp. chopped parsley
2 oz. mushrooms, chopped
salt and freshly ground black
    pepper
1 egg, beaten
a little single cream
$\frac{1}{2}$ pt. béchamel sauce
2 oz. white breadcrumbs
grated Parmesan cheese

SERVES 4

1 day ahead
Cook the cannelloni in plenty of boiling salted water for about 15 minutes and drain carefully. Dip the bread into the milk and squeeze it fairly dry. Place the bread in a basin, add the hard-boiled egg, parsley and mushrooms. Season and add the egg and enough cream to moisten the mixture. Carefully cut the cannelloni lengthwise, lay some stuffing along the centre of each and fold into their original form.

Lay them in a well buttered ovenproof dish, cover and refrigerate. Make the béchamel sauce.

About 30 minutes ahead
Coat the cannelloni with the béchamel sauce, sprinkle them first with dry breadcrumbs and then with grated Parmesan cheese and bake towards the top of the oven at 425°F, 220°C (mark 7) for about 15 minutes.

Chicken mille feuilles

8-oz. pkt. frozen puff pastry,
    thawed
8 oz. full fat cream cheese
2 tsps. lemon juice
4 level tsps. thick mayonnaise
$\frac{1}{4}$ level tsp. salt
freshly ground black pepper
12 oz. cooked chicken flesh
3–4 lettuce leaves, finely
    shredded
$\frac{1}{4}$ lb. firm tomatoes

SERVES 6

1 day (or more) ahead
Roll out the pastry into a rectangle 12 in. by 11 in. ($\frac{1}{4}$ in. thick). Prick it well and place on a dampened baking sheet. Divide equally into 3 crosswise and separate the pieces slightly. Place them on baking sheets and bake in the oven at 400°F, 200°C (mark 6) for 20–25 minutes until well risen. Cool on a wire rack. Store in an airtight tin.

In a bowl, using either a rotary whisk or an electric blender, blend together the cheese, lemon juice, mayonnaise and seasonings. Cut the chicken flesh into manageable pieces and add two-thirds to the creamed cheese mixture. Store covered in the refrigerator.

When required
Spread the chicken mixture lightly over the 3 pastry layers, and sprinkle shredded lettuce on top. Slice the tomatoes thinly, cut in half again and arrange over the lettuce. Layer up the pastry and chicken to form a loaf; top with remaining chicken and tomatoes. To serve, cut into thick slices with a really sharp knife.

Spiced shoulder of lamb

1 boned shoulder of lamb
1 level tbsp. dried rosemary
2 level tbsps. brown sugar
1 level tbsp. flour
1 level tsp. salt
½ level tsp. ground allspice
½ level tsp. ground ginger
pinch of nutmeg
2 oz. butter, melted
1 tbsp. vinegar
1 level tbsp. tomato ketchup

SERVES 4

2 days ahead
Flatten the lamb, make slits in the flesh and skin and insert spikes of rosemary. Combine the remaining ingredients and spread half over the fleshy surface. Roll up neatly and tie with fine string. Refrigerate, loosely wrapped in greaseproof paper.

1 day ahead
Unwrap and place the lamb in a roasting tin, pour the remaining spice mixture over and bake at 350°F, 180°C (mark 4) for about 1½ hours. Serve cold with mint jelly.

Spicy meat loaf

½ lb. beef, minced
¼ lb. sausage meat
¼ lb. lean bacon, rinded and minced
2 oz. fresh white breadcrumbs
6 oz. onion, skinned and chopped
¼ level tsp. mixed spice
1 level tsp. dried thyme
salt and pepper
1 egg
3 bayleaves

SERVES 4–6

1 day ahead
Mix together the beef, sausage meat and bacon. Add the breadcrumbs, onion, mixed spice, thyme, salt and pepper. Mix thoroughly, then bind with egg. Place the bayleaves in the bottom of a greased 1¼-pt. loaf tin. Spoon in the meat mixture and press well down. Cover with greased foil and refrigerate.

2 hours ahead
Place the tin on a baking sheet and bake in the oven at 325°F, 170°C (mark 3) for 2 hours. Turn it out of the tin. If required cold, allow to cool then refrigerate, wrapped in foil, until required – the same or next day.

Scotch eggs

6 hard-boiled eggs, shelled
1 oz. seasoned flour
1½ lb. sausage meat
1 egg, beaten
3 oz. fresh white breadcrumbs
oil for frying

SERVES 6

1 day ahead
Toss the eggs in flour. Divide the sausage meat into 4-oz. portions and on a lightly floured surface roll each piece into a circle large enough to cover an egg. Dust the surface with flour. Place an egg in the centre of each and shape the sausage meat round. Pinch the edges together and seal the joins with beaten egg. Brush evenly with egg, then toss in breadcrumbs. Press the crumbs well in. Store in a covered container in the refrigerator.

When required
Deep fry in oil at 340°F, 172°C, frying the eggs a few at a time for about 10 minutes until crisp

and golden brown. Drain on absorbent kitchen paper. If required cold, cook as soon as prepared then allow to cool and keep covered in the refrigerator until required. Serve with a salad.

Party chicken mould

$\frac{1}{2}$ a cooked chicken
2 eggs, hard-boiled
$\frac{3}{4}$ pt. well seasoned aspic jelly, made from aspic jelly powder and a dash of sherry
cooked peas

SERVES 8

1 day ahead
Cut the chicken into small pieces, removing all the bone and skin. Slice the eggs neatly. Wet a 2-pt. ring mould with straight sides, and coat it with aspic jelly. Set the peas round the base.

Dip each piece of egg in aspic jelly and position them round the side of the mould; leave in the refrigerator for a few minutes to set firmly. Fill up

Lasagne (*see page 35*)

Cannelloni au gratin *(see page 36)*

the mould with chicken and pour in the rest of the aspic. Leave in a cool place to set.

When required
Unmould just before serving.

Raised pie

¾ lb. lamb's liver
¾ lb. lean pork
1 lb. pork sausage meat
finely grated rind of 1 orange
2 tbsps. chopped parsley
⅛ level tsp. powdered cloves
½ level tsp. dried sage
2 level tsps. salt
freshly ground black pepper
½ pt. jellied stock or aspic
   jelly made from powdered
   aspic

For pastry
1 lb. plain flour
2 level tsps. salt
4 oz. lard
⅓ pt. water
beaten egg, to glaze

SERVES 8

1 day ahead
Mince the liver and pork; work them into the sausage meat with the orange rind, parsley, cloves, sage, salt and pepper.

Sift the flour and salt into a bowl. Melt the lard slowly in the water in a pan. Boil and pour it on to the flour. Work to a dough and knead. Grease a long loaf tin 13 in. by 4½ in. by 2½ in. (3½-pt. capacity) and line with two-thirds of the pastry. Spoon the meat into the centre and brush the pastry rim with beaten egg. Roll out the remaining pastry to make a lid. Seal the edges and use the trimmings for decoration. Make a hole in the centre. Brush with beaten egg. Bake at 400°F, 200°C (mark 6) for 20 minutes, then at 350°F, 180°C (mark 4) for about 1 hour 40 minutes. Remove the pie from the oven and when cold, pour well seasoned jellied stock or aspic jelly through the hole in the lid. Leave until set. Wrap and store in a cool place.

When required
Turn out of the tin and slice for serving.

Pork loaf

1 lb. raw lean pork, cubed
1 lb. raw lean ham, cubed
1 tbsp. finely chopped onion
¼ pt. thick white sauce
1 egg, beaten
salt and pepper
pinch of dried rosemary
thinly cut rashers of back
bacon, rinded
vinegar

SERVES 6

1 day ahead
Mince the pork, ham and onion twice. Blend these very thoroughly with the white sauce, egg, seasoning and rosemary and place the mixture on a sheet of kitchen foil. Form it into a loaf shape and cover with the rashers of bacon. Fold the foil over and seal the edges tightly. Place in a large pan of boiling water with a little vinegar and salt added and boil gently for 2½ hours. (A saucer placed on the base of the pan will prevent the foil coming directly into contact with the metal.)

Remove the loaf from the pan, leave to cool, and remove the foil. Re-wrap in greaseproof paper for refrigerator storage overnight.

When required
Slice thickly and serve with salad.

Cheese and salmon quiches

4 oz. shortcrust pastry (4 oz.
   plain flour, etc.)

1 egg

$\frac{1}{4}$ pt. milk

salt and pepper

$\frac{1}{2}$ medium onion, skinned and
   grated

3 oz. Cheddar cheese, grated

7 oz. can salmon (or tuna),
   drained and flaked

parsley sprigs for garnish

SERVES 4

1 day ahead
Roll out the pastry thinly and use it to line 4 individual 4-in. flan rings. Whisk together the egg, milk, salt and pepper. Add the onion and cheese. Mix well. Divide the salmon between the pastry cases and spoon the cheese custard over. Bake in the centre of the oven at 400°F, 200°C (mark 6) for 15 minutes, then reduce the temperature to 350°F, 180°C (mark 4) for a further 25 minutes until the quiches are golden brown and set. Cool quickly and refrigerate.

30 minutes ahead
Refresh in the oven at 350°F, 180°C (mark 4) for 20 minutes, then remove the rings. Keep warm – not hot. Serve garnished with sprigs of parsley.

3. Family Fare

Catering for the family on weekdays can often be more difficult to plan than a formal dinner party, especially when numbers, and mealtimes, vary from day to day. These recipes cover most eventualities – and likes and dislikes – and include hearty soups and chowders which, with crusty bread, are a meal in themselves.

If you make soup in advance, it's useful to know that it can mellow in taste if you keep it in the refrigerator for up to four days. But don't store soup with cream in it. The dairy ingredient should be added only when you're heating up the soup for serving.

You may need to add a little extra stock to thin soup down after it has been left to stand.

Fish chowder

$\frac{1}{4}$ lb. salt pork or green back bacon
$\frac{1}{4}$ lb. onions, skinned
$\frac{1}{2}$ lb. potatoes
$\frac{1}{2}$ oz. butter
$\frac{1}{2}$ lb. cod fillet, skinned
1 small bayleaf
$\frac{1}{2}$ pt. water
$\frac{1}{3}$ pt. milk
salt and pepper
1 tsp. lemon juice

SERVES 4

1 day ahead
Rind the pork and cut it into $\frac{1}{2}$-in. slices. Chop the onion. Keep onion and pork in plastic bags in the refrigerator. Peel the potatoes and keep them in a bowl of water in the refrigerator.

3 hours ahead
Fry the pork or bacon in a large saucepan until the fat begins to run. Add the butter and when melted add the skinned cod, cut into large cubes, discarding the bones. Dice the potatoes and stir in with onion, bayleaf and water. Cover, bring to the boil, reduce the heat and simmer for about $\frac{1}{2}$ hour until the potato is cooked. Set aside in a cool place.

10 minutes ahead
Reheat, then add the milk and seasoning including the lemon juice. Simmer for a further 5 minutes. Serve with crusty bread.

Curried cod chowder

$1\frac{1}{2}$ lb. cod fillet or any white
    fish
$1\frac{1}{2}$ pt. cold water
salt and freshly ground black
    pepper
8 oz. potato, peeled
2 oz. butter
6 oz. onion, skinned and
    chopped
6 oz. celery, wiped, trimmed
    and chopped
$\frac{1}{2}$ level tsp. mild curry powder
3 level tbsps. flour
$\frac{1}{2}$ pt. creamy milk
chopped parsley and chives
    for garnish

MAKES ABOUT $3\frac{1}{2}$ PT.

1 day ahead
Wipe the fish with a damp cloth. Place it in the base of a large saucepan, pour cold water over and season. Bring almost to the boil, remove from the heat and skim off the surface froth; carefully lift the fish, using a draining spoon, on to a plate. Remove skin and bones and flake into bite-sized portions. When cool, store covered in the refrigerator. Strain and reserve the fish stock. When cool, refrigerate it covered.

Cut the potatoes into small dice. Bring to the boil in salted water, cook until tender. Drain and reserve. When cool, store in a covered container in a cool place.

30 minutes ahead
Melt the butter in a large flameproof casserole. Stir in the onions and celery. Cook slowly until soft but not brown. Add the curry powder and flour and gradually blend in the fish stock and milk. Bring to the boil and cook for 2–3 minutes. Reduce the heat to a simmer before adding the potatoes and fish; check the seasoning. Garnish with chopped parsley and chives. Serve with warm French bread.

Easy tomato soup

4 oz. onion, skinned
3 cloves
2-lb. 3-oz. can tomatoes
sprig parsley
1 bayleaf
1 level tsp. salt
freshly ground black pepper
$\frac{1}{4}$ level tsp. freshly grated
    nutmeg
2 oz. butter
3 level tbsps. flour
$\frac{3}{4}$ pt. milk
$\frac{1}{4}$ pt. light stock
2–3 tbsps. single cream

MAKES ABOUT $2\frac{1}{2}$ PT.

1 day ahead
Cut the onions into small chunks and stud one piece with cloves. Place the onions, tomatoes with their juice, sprig of parsley, bayleaf, seasoning and nutmeg in a saucepan. Bring to the boil, reduce the heat, cover and simmer for 1 hour.

Melt the butter in another pan and blend in the flour. Cook the roux for 2–3 minutes before gradually stirring in the milk, to give a smooth paste. Bring to the boil, stirring. Reduce the heat and simmer for 5 minutes.

Remove the bayleaf, cloves and parsley from the tomato mixture and purée it in an electric blender. Pass the purée through a fine sieve to remove the tomato pips. Add it to the white sauce. Blend them well together, or combine both and liquidise together in the blender. Stir in the stock. Cool and store, covered, in the refrigerator.

When required
Check seasoning and stir in all but 1 tbsp. of the

cream. Heat gently, without boiling. Just before serving pour the remaining cream into the soup and stir gently to swirl the cream.

Beef broth with pasta

4 oz. leeks
4 oz. onions, skinned
2 pt. rich beef stock
1 tsp. Worcestershire sauce
$\frac{1}{2}$ tsp. gravy browning
$\frac{1}{4}$ level tsp. mixed herbs
salt and pepper
8 oz. minced beef
2 oz. fresh white breadcrumbs
$\frac{1}{4}$ level tsp. mixed herbs
$1\frac{1}{2}$ level tsps. salt
freshly ground black pepper
2 oz. pasta cartwheel shapes

MAKES ABOUT 3 PT.

1 day ahead
Trim the leeks and cut them in fine shreds; wash well and drain. Dice the onion and combine with the leeks in a large saucepan. Pour in the stock, add the Worcestershire sauce, gravy browning, herbs and seasoning. Bring to the boil, reduce the heat, cover and simmer for about 20 minutes. Cool and store in a cool place.

Re-mince the beef to give a really fine texture. Combine with breadcrumbs, herbs and seasoning. Shape into small balls about the size of a marble. Store, covered, in the refrigerator.

45 minutes ahead
Place the meatballs in the broth and pour it over the pasta. Bring to the boil, reduce the heat and simmer, covered, for about 30 minutes, stirring from time to time. Serve with oven warm bread.

Cream of carrot and lettuce soup

$1\frac{1}{2}$ lb. carrots
2 pt. veal bone stock
salt and freshly ground black
    pepper
2 oz. bacon rashers, rinded
1 oz. butter
1 small lettuce
1 oz. vermicelli

1–2 days ahead
Pare the carrots and slice thickly. Place them in a large saucepan with $1\frac{1}{2}$ pt. stock and seasoning. Bring to the boil, reduce the heat, cover and simmer until the carrots are tender – about 45 minutes. Purée them in an electric blender, including the stock.

Meanwhile, snip the bacon into very small dice using kitchen scissors. Melt the butter in a clean pan, add the bacon and fry slowly until the bacon is slightly browned. Trim the lettuce and chop it with a stainless steel knife. Add it to the pan, stir and add the puréed carrot and $\frac{1}{2}$ pt. stock. Cool and store, covered, in the refrigerator.

15 minutes ahead
Bring to the boil, sprinkle in vermicelli, adjust seasoning and cook for 10 minutes.

Chunky courgette soup

4 oz. haricot beans
salt
12 oz. potatoes
8 oz. courgettes, trimmed
12 oz. leeks, washed
1 clove garlic, skinned and
    crushed
2 tbsps. oil
2 oz. butter
2 pt. chicken or veal stock
freshly ground black pepper
$\frac{1}{2}$ level tsp. dried basil
4 oz. Cheddar cheese, grated
chopped parsley

MAKES ABOUT $3\frac{1}{2}$ PT.

2–3 days ahead
Soak the beans overnight in water. Next day, drain and place the beans in a saucepan; cover with salted fresh water and simmer, covered, for $1\frac{1}{2}$ hours. Drain. Peel and dice the potatoes, slice the courgettes into chunky slices about $\frac{1}{4}$-in. thick. Chop the leeks finely and combine the garlic with the leeks. Heat the oil; fry the potato first for 2–3 minutes. Drain it, using a slotted spoon; and place it in a large saucepan. Next sauté the leeks for about 5 minutes, stirring frequently; drain and add to the potato. Lastly, melt the butter, add the courgettes and cook for about 5 minutes. Add these to the pan with the beans. Pour over the stock and add the seasoning and basil. Simmer, covered, for $1\frac{1}{4}$ hours until the vegetables are tender. Cool and store, covered, in the refrigerator.

20 minutes ahead
Reheat, and when at simmering point sprinkle the cheese over the soup. Continue simmering for another 15 minutes. Check seasoning, Garnish with chopped parsley.

Cream of artichoke soup

2 lb. Jerusalem artichokes
2 slices of lemon
$1\frac{1}{2}$ pt. cold water
1 oz. butter
4 oz. onion, skinned and
    chopped
2 level tbsps. cornflour
$\frac{3}{4}$ pt. milk
$1\frac{1}{2}$ tbsps. lemon juice
2 tbsps. chopped parsley
$1\frac{1}{2}$ level tsps. salt
white pepper
$2\frac{1}{2}$ fl. oz. single cream

MAKES ABOUT $2\frac{1}{4}$ PT.

1 day ahead
Wash the artichokes well. Place them in a large saucepan with the lemon slices, cover with water and bring to the boil. Reduce the heat, cover and simmer until the artichokes are tender – about 20 minutes. Drain off the water and reserve 1 pt. Allow the artichokes to cool then peel away the skins and mash them roughly. Melt the butter in a clean saucepan, add the onion and fry until soft but not coloured. Stir in the cornflour, reserved artichoke water and milk. Stir in the mashed artichokes. Bring the sauce to the boil, stirring, and cook for 2–3 minutes then remove from the heat and purée in an electric blender. Cool and store in the refrigerator.

10 minutes ahead
Reheat the soup in a saucepan. Stir in the lemon juice, parsley, seasoning and cream. Bring to serving temperature and garnish with croûtons.

Lentil pepperpot

8 oz. lentils

1½ oz. butter

4 oz. onion, skinned and
   chopped

6½-oz. can pimiento, drained
   and chopped

4 oz. green pepper, seeded and
   diced

2 level tbsps. flour

15-oz. can tomatoes

2¼ pt. chicken stock

6 oz. carrots, peeled and thinly
   sliced

2 level tsps. salt

freshly ground black pepper

chopped parsley

MAKES ABOUT 3½ PT.

Up to 4 days ahead

Soak the lentils overnight. Melt the butter in a
large saucepan or flameproof casserole and sauté
the onion, pimiento and pepper until soft but not
coloured – about 5 minutes. Stir in the flour and
cook for a further 1–2 minutes. Drain the tomatoes
and dice the flesh; reserve the juice. Stir the stock
gradually into the pan, then add the tomatoes and
juice, carrots, salt, pepper, and drained lentils.
Cover and simmer over low heat for 2 hours. Stir
occasionally. Cool and refrigerate, covered.

10 minutes ahead

Reheat the soup in a pan, stirring occasionally.
Check seasoning before garnishing with chopped
parsley.

Oxtail soup with mustard dumplings

1 oxtail (2 lb.) chopped into
   small pieces

2 tbsps. oil

4 oz. celery, diced

4 oz. carrot, diced

1 small turnip, diced

3 pt. rich beef stock

1 level tsp. salt

freshly ground black pepper

bouquet garni

½ tsp. gravy browning

¾ level tsp. concentrated curry
   sauce

½–¾ pt. beef stock

For dumplings

3 oz. self-raising flour

¾ level tsp. dry mustard

1½ oz. shredded suet

½ level tsp. salt

freshly ground black pepper

water

MAKES ABOUT 3 PT.

Up to 3 days ahead

Wipe the oxtail with a damp cloth. Remove any
excess fat. Place the meat in a frying pan with the
oil and fry briskly to seal the surfaces. Drain and
place in a large saucepan. Fry the vegetables in
the reheated meat residue for 3–4 minutes then add
them to the meat. Pour over the stock, season well,
add a bouquet garni, cover and simmer for 4 hours.

Strain the soup and discard the bouquet garni.
Chill the meat juices to allow all the fat to set and
remove the fat. Take all the meat from the bones,
heat the meat, juices and vegetables together and
purée them twice in an electric blender. Return
the purée to the pan and stir in the last 3 ingredients. Bring to the boil, reduce the heat,
check the seasoning, cool and store covered in the
refrigerator.

1 hour ahead

Sift the self-raising flour and dry mustard together,
stir in the suet, salt and pepper. Add water and
mix to give a firm dough. Shape into about 20
small balls.

Reheat the soup to boiling point, reduce to
simmering and add the dumplings. Cook for about
30 minutes.

Chunky courgette soup (*see page 45*)

Potato and leek soup

12 oz. leeks
1 oz. butter or margarine
1½ lb. potatoes
3 pt. light stock
bouquet garni
salt and freshly ground black
  pepper
French bread
grated cheese
chopped parsley

MAKES ABOUT 3¾ PT.

1 day ahead
Discard a third of the green top from the leeks. Slice the remainder finely and wash it thoroughly. Drain and place with 1 oz. butter in a large saucepan; cover and sauté for 5 minutes. Meanwhile, peel and roughly dice the potatoes and add to the pan with the stock, bouquet garni and seasoning. Bring to the boil, reduce the heat, cover and simmer for about 1 hour until the potatoes are soft. Discard the bouquet garni. Purée the vegetables in an electric blender or pass through a sieve. Cool and keep covered in the refrigerator.

About 15 minutes ahead
Return the soup to the pan; thin it down with a little extra stock, if you wish. Bring to serving temperature and adjust seasoning. Meanwhile slice some French bread, top with grated cheese and grill. Garnish the soup with chopped parsley and serve with the cheese-topped bread.

Thick pea and ham potage

4 oz. split green peas
salt
2 oz. butter or margarine
6 oz. celery, washed and sliced
6 oz. potatoes, peeled and
  sliced
2 oz. onion, skinned and diced
6 oz. leeks, trimmed and finely
  sliced
1 tbsp. chopped parsley
1 level tbsp. flour
2 pt. chicken stock
freshly ground black pepper
¼–½ lb. ham, in a piece, diced
chopped parsley

MAKES ABOUT 3 PT.

2 days ahead
Soak the peas overnight (don't use the white soaking tablet generally supplied with them).

1 day ahead
Drain the peas then cover with fresh water to which ¼ level tsp. salt has been added. Bring to the boil, boil for 2–3 minutes, then reduce the heat, cover and cook for about 1 hour until soft. Melt the butter or margarine add the celery, potato, onion, well washed leek and parsley. Cook, covered, until the vegetables are tender but not coloured. Stir in the flour, cook for 1–2 minutes then gradually blend in the stock, 2 level tsps. salt and a little pepper. Bring to the boil, reduce the heat, cover, and simmer for about 30 minutes. Drain the peas and add them to the other vegetables. Stir through, then purée the mixture in an electric blender in convenient amounts. Cool and refrigerate.

About 10 minutes ahead
Reheat the soup, with ham added, to serving temperature. Garnish with parsley.

Vegetable broth

1½ oz. butter
8 oz. onion, skinned and
    chopped
8 oz. leeks, trimmed and finely
    sliced
1 small red pepper, seeded
    and diced
1 small green pepper, seeded
    and diced
8 oz. carrots, pared and diced
2 pt. stock
½ pt. milk
1 bayleaf
salt and freshly ground black
    pepper
1 level tbsp. cornflour
chopped parsley

SERVES 6

1 day ahead
Heat the butter in a large pan; add the onions, cover and fry until transparent. Add the leeks, peppers and carrots to the pan, stir well, cover and cook over a fairly high heat for 10 minutes. Gradually add the stock, milk and bayleaf. Cover and simmer for 15–20 minutes. Season to taste. Cool and store, covered, in a cool place.

About 15 minutes ahead
Bring the soup to simmering point. Meanwhile, mix the cornflour with a little water to a smooth cream. Add a little of the hot soup and then stir it into the bulk. Bring to the boil, stirring all the time. Serve garnished with plenty of chopped parsley.

Canadian cheese soup

½ lb. potatoes, peeled
½ lb. onions, skinned
2 oz. carrots, pared
2 oz. celery, diced
½ pt. water
1 pt. rich turkey or chicken
    stock
¼ lb. mature Cheddar cheese
3 tbsps. single cream
salt and pepper
2 tbsps. chopped parsley

MAKES ABOUT 3 PT.

1 day ahead
Finely slice or dice the potatoes, onion and carrot. Place them in a saucepan with the celery and water. Bring to the boil, reduce the heat, cover and simmer for about 20 minutes until the vegetables are tender. Cool and store in the refrigerator.

About 10 minutes ahead
Add the rest of the ingredients except the parsley and reheat without boiling. Adjust seasoning, sprinkle in the parsley and serve.

Steak and kidney pudding

¼ lb. kidney, skinned and
    cored
1 lb. stewing steak, cut into
    ½-in. cubes
2 level tbsps. seasoned flour
1 onion, skinned and chopped
8 oz. suetcrust pastry (8 oz.
    flour, etc.)

SERVES 4

1 day ahead
Slice the kidney and coat both the steak and kidney with seasoned flour. Place in a casserole with the chopped onion and 2–3 tbsps. water. Cover and cook in the oven at 350°F, 180°C (mark 4) for 2 hours. Cool quickly and store in the refrigerator. Make the pastry, wrap it in greaseproof paper and refrigerate.

2 hours ahead
Half-fill a steamer or large saucepan with water

49

and put it on to boil. Grease a 1½-pt. pudding basin. Cut off a quarter of the pastry to make a lid. Roll out the remainder and use it to line the basin. Fill the lined basin with the cooked meat mixture.

Roll out the remaining quarter of the pastry to a round the size of the basin top and damp the edge of it. Place on top of the pudding and seal the edges of the pastry well. Cover with greased greaseproof paper or foil and steam over rapidly boiling water, refilling the pan as necessary with boiling water. Serve from the basin.

Chilli con carne

1 lb. minced beef
1 large onion, skinned and finely sliced
½ level tsp. chilli powder
1 level tsp. salt
pinch paprika pepper
1-lb. 13-oz. can tomatoes
16-oz. can red kidney beans, drained

SERVES 4–6

1 day ahead
Brown the meat in a large saucepan for 5 minutes, without any extra fat. Add the onion and seasonings, blending them well together. Add the tomatoes, bring to the boil, cover and simmer for 1½–2 hours. Cool and refrigerate, covered.

About 30 minutes ahead
Bring the meat back to the boil, stirring, then add the beans and cook gently for a further 15–20 minutes. Serve in bowls and eat with spoons, with French bread.

Shepherd's pie

1 lb. potatoes, peeled
2 tbsps. milk
½ oz. butter
salt and pepper
1 onion, skinned and chopped
a little dripping
8 oz. cooked cold beef, minced
stock
1 tbsp. chopped parsley, or 1 level tsp. dried mixed herbs

SERVES 4

1 day ahead
Boil the potatoes, drain and mash them with the milk, butter and seasoning. Keep covered in a cool place. Fry the onion in a little dripping for about 5 minutes and mix in the minced meat, with a little stock, seasoning and parsley or mixed herbs. Put the prepared meat mixture into an ovenproof dish. Cool and cover. Store in the refrigerator.

45 minutes ahead
Cover the top of the meat mixture with mashed potato. Mark the top with a fork and bake for 25–30 minutes in the top of the oven at 375°F, 190°C (mark 5), until the surface is crisp and browned.

Variations
1. Add a small can of tomatoes, drained and chopped, to the meat/onion mixture.

Cream of artichoke soup (*see page 45*)

2. Mix 1–2 tbsps. pickle with the meat or put it in a layer at the bottom of the dish.

3. Top the mashed potatoes with a little grated cheese before baking the pie.

Goulash

1½ lb. stewing steak
2 oz. lard
1 medium onion, skinned and chopped
1–2 level tbsps. paprika pepper
1 level tbsp. tomato paste
just under ½ pt. beef stock, made from a cube
½ oz. cornflour
2 tbsps. water
2½ fl. oz. soured cream

SERVES 4

1–2 days ahead
Wipe, trim and cube the beef; fry it in hot lard until brown on all sides. Add the onion and cook for 2–3 minutes. Stir in the paprika, tomato paste and beef stock, bring to the boil then transfer to a casserole. Cover and cook in the centre of the oven at 325°F, 170°C (mark 3) for 1½ hours. Cool quickly and refrigerate.

1 hour ahead
Place the goulash in the oven at 375°F, 190°C (mark 5) for about 45 minutes, to reheat.

5 minutes ahead
Blend ½ oz. cornflour with 2 tbsps. water and stir into the hot goulash to thicken it. Serve the soured cream separately, or spoon some on to each helping.

Steak and mushroom pie

1 lb. stewing steak
2 level tbsps. seasoned flour
1 onion, skinned and thinly sliced
water
4 oz. mushrooms, sliced
1 pkt. puff pastry – 4–6 oz., according to size of dish
egg to glaze

SERVES 4

1 day ahead
Wipe the meat, cut it into small, even pieces and coat it with seasoned flour. Put the meat and onions into a pan and just cover with water. Bring to the boil, reduce the heat and simmer for 1½–2 hours or until the meat is tender. (Or you can cook the meat for 2 hours in a covered casserole in the centre of the oven at 350°F, 180°C, mark 4.) Cool and refrigerate, covered, until required.

1 hour ahead
Put the meat and mushrooms into a pie dish with enough of the gravy to half-fill it. Roll out the pastry 1 in. larger than the top of the dish. Cut off a ½-in. strip from round the edge of the pastry and put the strip round the dampened rim of the dish. Damp the edges of the pastry with water and place on top of the pie, without stretching the pastry. Trim if necessary and flake the edges. Decorate it if you like with the trimmings and brush with beaten egg. Bake near the top of the oven at 425°F, 220°C (mark 7), for 20 minutes.

Then reduce the heat to 350°F, 180°C (mark 4) and cook for about a further 20 minutes.

Variations
Replace the mushrooms with 4 oz. lamb's kidneys; wipe and core, removing any skin, cut into small pieces, and add them to the meat in the pie dish before covering with the pastry.

Cornish pasties

12 oz. chuck or blade steak
4 oz. potato, peeled and diced
1 small onion, skinned and
    chopped
salt and pepper
12 oz. shortcrust pastry (12 oz.
    flour, etc.)

SERVES 4

1 day ahead
Cut the steak into small pieces; add the potato and onion and season well. Divide the pastry into four and roll out each piece into a round about 8 in. in diameter. Divide the meat mixture between the pastry rounds, damp the edges and draw the edges of the pastry together to form a seam across the top. Flute the seam with your fingers. Place the pasties on a baking tray and refrigerate.

When required
Bake at the top of the oven at 425°F, 220°C (mark 7) for 15 minutes to brown the pastry, then reduce the heat to 325°F, 170°C (mark 3) and cook for a further hour. Serve hot or cold.

Casseroled kidneys

1 lb. lamb's kidneys
1 oz. lard or dripping
3 small onions, skinned and
    finely chopped
½ oz. seasoned flour
salt and pepper
4 rashers back bacon, rinded
    and diced
⅓ pt. stock
1½ lb. potatoes, boiled and
    creamed
beaten egg or melted butter to
    glaze
chopped parsley

SERVES 4

1 day ahead
Clean the kidneys, halve them and remove the cores and skin. Place them in cold water, bring to the boil and throw away the water. Repeat twice. Melt the lard in a frying pan and fry the onions until light golden brown. Stir in the flour and place them in a casserole. Arrange the kidneys on top of the onions; season with salt and pepper. Top with small pieces of bacon and pour the stock over. Cover the casserole and cook in the oven at 350°F, 180°C (mark 4) for about 30 minutes until the kidneys are tender. Cool and refrigerate, covered, until required. Boil and cream the potatoes. Cover and keep in a cool place.

20 minutes ahead
Line a heatproof dish with the creamed potatoes and brush with egg or butter. Brown in the oven at 400°F, 200°C (mark 6) or under the grill. Reheat the kidney mixture in a strong saucepan or flameproof casserole, allowing it to simmer for

5 minutes, stirring occasionally and adding a little more stock or water if needed. To serve, place the kidney mixture in the potato-lined dish; sprinkle with chopped parsley.

Pigaleekie

½ oz. butter
1 lb. lean pork, minced
1 clove garlic, skinned and crushed
½ lb. leeks, washed and cut into large dice
1 small red pepper, seeded and finely diced
¾ pt. stock
salt and pepper
5 level tbsps. long grain rice
gravy browning (optional)
chopped parsley

SERVES 4

1 day ahead
Heat the butter in a shallow flameproof casserole, stir in the pork and cook quickly for 5 minutes. Drain off the fat. Add the garlic, leeks, red pepper and stock. Season well, cover and cook in the oven at 325°F, 170°C (mark 3) for 1 hour. Cool and store, covered, in the refrigerator.

30 minutes ahead
Reheat in a saucepan on the top of the stove. When bubbling, stir in the rice and simmer for a further 15–20 minutes. Adjust colouring, if necessary, with a little gravy browning. Sprinkle liberally with chopped parsley just before serving.

Mild lamb curry

1 oz. butter
3 oz. onion, skinned and chopped
1 stick celery, chopped
2 oz. mushrooms, sliced
2 level tsps. curry powder
2 level tsps. tomato paste
1 level tbsp. flour
1 level tbsp. mango chutney
½ pt. brown stock
1 oz. sultanas
8 oz. cold roast lamb, chopped
1 small banana, sliced
1 oz. salted peanuts and chopped parsley for garnish

SERVES 2

Up to 3 days ahead
Melt the butter in a saucepan and fry the onion until transparent. Add celery and mushrooms and cook for a further 2 minutes. Stir in the curry powder, tomato paste, flour and chutney, and cook for a further 2 minutes. Add the stock gradually, stirring, and bring to the boil to thicken. Add the sultanas and lamb. Adjust seasoning, cover, and simmer for 30 minutes.

15 minutes ahead
Reheat the curry in a saucepan and when bubbling add the banana. Simmer for a further 5 minutes. Serve garnished with peanuts and parsley.

Casseroled kidneys (*see page 53*)

Sausage pie

½ lb. pork sausages or sausage
  meat
1 oz. dripping
1 onion, skinned and thinly
  sliced
2 tomatoes, peeled and sliced
1 apple, peeled, cored and
  chopped
1 potato, peeled and diced
salt and pepper
4 oz. shortcrust pastry (4 oz.
  flour, etc.)

SERVES 2

1 day ahead
Remove the sausage skins and divide each sausage
into two, or shape the sausage meat into 8 balls.
Melt the dripping and lightly fry all the ingredients, except the seasoning and pastry, until
beginning to brown. Turn them into a 1¼-pt. oval
pie dish. Season, leave until cool, then store,
covered, in the refrigerator.

About 1 hour ahead
Roll out the pastry and cover the pie. Place the
dish on a baking sheet and bake in the oven at
400°F, 200°C (mark 6) for about 30 minutes.

Cheddar eggs

1 lb. potatoes, peeled
1 egg, beaten
½ oz. butter
2 oz. mature Cheddar cheese,
    grated
salt and pepper
2 oz. cooked lean ham,
    chopped
2 oz. processed cheese,
    chopped
flour
fresh white breadcrumbs
oil for deep frying

SERVES 4

1 day ahead
Cook the potatoes in salted water until tender. Drain and mash them with 1 tbsp. egg, butter, grated cheese and seasoning. Cool the potato. Combine the ham and chopped cheese. Form the potato into 4 rounds, using floured hands and place a quarter of the ham and cheese in the centre of each; form them into egg shapes and coat first in the remaining egg and then breadcrumbs. Store, covered, in the refrigerator.

10 minutes ahead
Deep fry for about 5 minutes until crisp and golden brown. Drain and serve with a sharply dressed tomato salad.

Pasta niçoise

4 oz. twisted pasta
2 firm tomatoes
2 eggs, hardboiled
4-oz. can tuna, drained
½ red pepper, seeded and finely
    sliced
2 oz. French beans, cooked
8 black olives
few capers
3 tbsps. garlic flavoured
    French dressing

SERVES 2

1 day ahead
Cook the pasta in boiling salted water until tender but not soft. Drain it well and rinse at once in cold water. Cool. Store, covered, in a cool place.

About 30 minutes ahead
Quarter the tomatoes, shell and cut the hard-boiled eggs lengthwise into quarters. Flake the tuna. Place the pasta, fish, tomatoes, sliced red pepper, French beans, olives and capers in a bowl and mix gently.

Just before serving
Add the French dressing and toss the salad, using two forks. Spoon it on to a serving dish or 2 individual plates; garnish with the quartered hard-boiled eggs. Serve with crusty French bread.

Fish cakes

¾ lb. cooked fish, flaked
½ lb. sieved cooked potatoes
¼ pt. parsley sauce
salt and pepper
a little flour
egg and breadcrumbs
fat for frying
lemon and parsley or water-
    cress to garnish

SERVES 4

1 day ahead
Mix together the fish, potatoes, sauce and the seasoning and put aside to cool. Form the mixture into flat cakes, using a little flour and coat them with egg and breadcrumbs.

When required
Fry the fish cakes in hot fat until evenly browned. Garnish with lemon and parsley or watercress.

Cod au gratin

1 fillet of cod (about $\frac{3}{4}$ lb.)
$\frac{1}{2}$ oz. butter
$\frac{1}{2}$ oz. flour
$\frac{1}{2}$ pt. milk
4 oz. Cheddar cheese, grated
grated rind and juice of $\frac{1}{2}$
   lemon
salt and freshly ground black
   pepper
3-oz. pkt. instant potato
milk to mix
lemon wedges for garnish

SERVES 2

1 day ahead
Skin the fish and poach it for 10 minutes in simmering water. Drain and store, covered, in the refrigerator when cold. Make a white sauce; melt the butter in a pan, add the flour and cook for a few minutes; off the heat, pour on the milk a little at a time, mixing well. Return the pan to the heat and, stirring continuously, bring to the boil. Add grated cheese, lemon rind and juice. Season, cover and keep in a cool place.

1 hour ahead
Make up the potato as directed on the packet. Season and add enough milk to give a piping consistency. When sufficiently cool, spoon the potato into a piping bag fitted with a star vegetable nozzle. Pipe a border of potato round a shallow ovenproof dish and put it under a hot grill to brown.

Flake the fish into large pieces and place it in the potato-bordered dish. Reheat the white sauce and pour it over the fish. Place it in the centre of the oven at 350°F, 180°C (mark 4) and cook for about 30 minutes. Serve garnished with lemon wedges.

Topcrust vegetable pie

$\frac{1}{2}$ lb. onions, skinned
$\frac{1}{2}$ lb. leeks, trimmed
$\frac{1}{2}$ lb. carrots, pared
$\frac{1}{2}$ lb. turnips, peeled
3 oz. butter or margarine
$\frac{1}{4}$ pt. water
$\frac{3}{4}$ pt. milk, approx.
$\frac{1}{2}$ lb. tomatoes, peeled
$15\frac{1}{2}$-oz. can butter beans,
   drained
salt and pepper
2 tbsps. chopped parsley
$1\frac{1}{2}$ oz. flour
6 oz. mature Cheddar cheese,
   grated
8 oz. shortcrust pastry (8 oz.
   flour, etc.)

SERVES 4–5

1 day ahead
Prepare the vegetables: roughly chop the onions; leave some green on the leeks, cut them into $\frac{1}{4}$-in. slices and then wash thoroughly; cut the carrots into matchsticks; dice the turnips. Melt $1\frac{1}{2}$ oz. butter or margarine in a pan and add these vegetables, letting them 'sweat' in the butter, covered with a lid, for 10 minutes. Add $\frac{1}{4}$ pt. water and simmer for a further 10 minutes. Drain the vegetables and make the juices up to $\frac{3}{4}$ pt. with milk.

Layer up the sweated vegetables with halved tomatoes and butter beans in a $3\frac{1}{2}$-pt. pie dish, adding seasoning between the layers. Add parsley; if necessary, place a pie funnel among the vegetables to fill the dish well. Put the remaining fat in a clean pan and heat gently. When melted, stir in the flour and cook it for 1–2 minutes. Off the heat, gradually beat in the milk and vegetable juices. Bring to the boil, and boil for 1–2 minutes.

Stir in the cheese, adjust the seasoning and pour the sauce over the vegetables. Allow to cool and store, covered in the refrigerator. Make up the pastry and store it, covered, in the refrigerator.

1 hour ahead
Roll out the pastry and cover the filling with a pastry lid. Place on a baking sheet and bake in the oven at 400°F, 200°C (mark 6) for about 45 minutes.

Curried rice salad

4 level tbsps. thick
   mayonnaise
$\frac{1}{2}$–1 level tsp. curry paste
little grated orange rind
freshly ground black pepper
2 rings of canned pineapple
4 oz. cooked long grain rice
4 oz. sliced ham or cooked
   white chicken meat
parsley

SERVES 2

1 day ahead
Combine the mayonnaise, curry paste and orange rind with pepper to taste.

15 minutes ahead
Cut the pineapple into thin pieces – using a sharp knife or scissors – and fold into half the mayonnaise with the rice. Arrange the rice in a bed on a flat dish. With scissors, cut the ham or chicken into julienne strips and fold these through the remaining mayonnaise. Pile on to the rice and garnish with scissor-snipped parsley.

Bubble and squeak bake

2 lb. old potatoes, peeled
butter
milk
salt and pepper
1 lb. firm green cabbage,
   quartered
$\frac{1}{2}$ lb. onions, skinned
$\frac{1}{2}$ lb. carrots, pared
6 oz. mature Cheddar cheese

SERVES 4–6

1 day ahead
Cook the potatoes in boiling salted water until tender. Drain and cream them with a knob of butter and a little milk. Season well.

Cook the cabbage, drain it well and chop. Finely chop the onion and grate the carrots; turn these into boiling salted water, cook for 5 minutes, then drain. Blend the cabbage and potato. Turn half into a buttered shallow 9-in. diameter ($1\frac{3}{4}$-pt.) baking dish. Cover with onion and carrot and top with 4 oz. grated cheese. Spread the vegetables evenly and top with the remaining potato mixture. Smooth the surface with a knife, mark it with a fork and grate the remainder of the cheese over the top. Store covered in the refrigerator.

About 45 minutes ahead
Bake in the oven at 400°F, 200°C (mark 6) until golden brown. Serve in wedges.

4. Soups and Starters

Interesting starters don't necessarily call for last-minute complications. Potted smoked salmon (by no means as expensive as it may sound!), mushrooms à la grecque, and taramasalata are just a few of the cook-ahead ideas here. Soups – chilled as well as piping hot – are included (refer to Chapter 3 as well). Dress up creamed soup before serving; a pat of butter or a dollop of thick cream in each bowl appeals to the eye as well as to the palate. For a garnish, use chopped fresh herbs, such as parsley, chives, or basil, or leaves of watercress.

So far as pâtés are concerned, you'll find that most of them – apart from delicate fish ones – will keep quite happily for a week in the refrigerator; in fact this can even improve the flavour.

Crème vichyssoise (*see page 60*)

Cream of onion soup

4 oz. onion, skinned and thinly
  sliced
1½ oz. butter
¾ oz. flour
1 pt. milk, hot
½ pt. stock
salt and pepper
2 egg yolks
2 tbsps. single cream
chopped parsley for garnish

SERVES 4

1 day ahead

Sauté the onions in the butter until soft but not coloured. Stir in the flour and cook for about 3 minutes. Slowly stir in the milk – hot, but not boiling – and ½ pt. stock. Adjust seasoning. Simmer for 15–20 minutes then cool and store, covered, in the refrigerator.

15 minutes ahead

Reheat to simmering point in a saucepan. Blend the egg yolks with the cream. Stir in a little of the hot soup and pour it into the pan. Reheat the soup without boiling. Garnish with parsley and serve toasted croûtons separately.

Crème vichyssoise

3 medium leeks
1 small onion, skinned
1 oz. butter
1 lb. potatoes, peeled
1½ pt. white stock
salt and pepper
1 egg yolk
¼ pt. single cream
chives

SERVES 4–6

1 day ahead

Prepare the leeks, cutting off most of the green tops. Slice the leeks and onion thinly. Melt the butter in a saucepan, add the leeks and onion and sauté without browning for 5 minutes. Add the roughly chopped potatoes, stock and seasoning. Bring to the boil, cover and simmer for about 30 minutes then sieve or purée it in an electric blender. Allow to cool and store covered in the refrigerator.

15 minutes ahead

Reheat the soup to simmering point. Blend the egg yolk with the cream, stir in a little hot soup then add it to the soup in the pan. Heat again without boiling and adjust the seasoning. Serve with a garnish of snipped chives.

Chilled tomato soup

½ lb. onions, skinned and
  chopped
2 tbsps. oil
1 lb. tomatoes, quartered
¼ level tsp. paprika pepper
10½-oz. can condensed
  consommé
¼ pt. double cream

SERVES 6

1–2 days ahead

Cook the onions in the oil until tender but not coloured. Stir in the tomatoes, cover with a lid and simmer gently for 20 minutes. Stir in the paprika and condensed soup. Purée in a blender and pass through a sieve. Add a can of cold water. Chill. Store in the refrigerator.

5 minutes ahead

Adjust the seasoning and ladle the soup into individual bowls. Put 1 tbsp. cream into each bowl and whirl the cream with a teaspoon.

Lettuce and onion soup (*see below*)

Lettuce and onion soup

2 oz. butter
1 large onion, skinned and
   finely chopped
1 large lettuce, washed and
   finely shredded
2 pt. chicken stock
salt and pepper
2.75-fl. oz. carton double
   cream

SERVES 6

1 day ahead
Heat the butter in a saucepan; add the onion and
fry gently until soft; don't allow it to colour.
Add the lettuce and cook it in the butter for a
few minutes, then add the stock and seasoning.
Bring to the boil, cover and simmer for 5–7
minutes. Place half in an electric blender and blend
until smooth. Turn it into a bowl and repeat
with remainder. Cool and refrigerate, covered.

About 15 minutes ahead
Return the mixture to the saucepan. Bring to the
boil, then remove from the heat and gradually add
the cream, stirring all the time. Serve hot with
cheese straws.

Chilled cream of spinach soup

1 lb. spinach
2 oz. butter
1 onion, skinned and chopped
1½ pt. chicken stock
¼ level tsp. salt
freshly ground black pepper
2 tsps. lemon juice
1 bayleaf
½ oz. flour
croûtons of fried bread
4 tbsps. single cream
grated cheese, for croûtons

SERVES 4–6

1 day ahead
Wash and drain the spinach and discard the stalks. In a large pan, melt half the butter and sauté the onion until soft but not coloured. Add the spinach and sauté for a further 5 minutes, stirring frequently. Add the stock, salt, pepper, lemon juice and bayleaf. Bring to the boil, cover and simmer for about 15 minutes. Discard the bayleaf and sieve the soup or purée it in a blender.

In a clean pan, make a roux with the rest of the butter and the flour. Slowly add the soup, stirring. Bring to the boil and simmer for 5 minutes. Adjust seasoning. Turn into a bowl and refrigerate, covered. Make the croûtons. Drain on absorbent kitchen paper. When cool, keep in an airtight container.

10 minutes ahead
Pour the soup into soup cups and add a little cream to each cup. Sprinkle grated cheese on the croûtons and hand round separately.

Chilled cucumber soup

1 small onion, skinned and
    sliced
1½ pt. white stock
1 large or 2 small cucumbers
sprig of mint
1 level tbsp. cornflour
2–3 tbsps. cream
salt and pepper
edible green colouring

SERVES 4

1 day ahead
Simmer the onion for 15 minutes in a pan with the stock. Peel and chop the cucumber (saving a little for garnish) and add to the stock with the mint; simmer for about 20 minutes, or until the cucumber is cooked. Sieve the soup or purée it in an electric blender; return it to the pan and reheat. Blend the cornflour with a little cold water to a smooth cream. Stir in a little of the hot soup, return the mixture to the pan, and bring to the boil, stirring until it thickens. Cook for a further 2–3 minutes. Cool and store, covered, in the refrigerator.

A few hours ahead
Reheat, and when bubbling remove from the heat and stir in the cream. Re-season if necessary. Tint the soup delicately with green colouring. Pour it into a large bowl, cover and chill.

When required
Serve it with 2 or 3 slices of cucumber floating

on top, and serve cheese straws as an accompaniment.

Peter's pâté

1 lb. pig's liver
2 oz. butter
1 onion, skinned and chopped
$\frac{1}{4}$ lb. streaky bacon, rinded and diced
$\frac{1}{4}$ lb. belly pork, diced
1 clove garlic
$1\frac{1}{2}$ level tbsps. tomato paste
$\frac{1}{8}$ level tsp. black pepper
$\frac{1}{8}$ level tsp. garlic salt
$\frac{1}{8}$ level tsp. dried basil
$\frac{1}{8}$ level tsp. salt
4 tbsps. red wine
grated rind of $\frac{1}{4}$ lemon
1 bayleaf
lettuce, cucumber and tomato for garnish

SERVES 8

1–2 days ahead
Remove the skin and any gristle from the liver. Melt the butter and fry the onion. Add the remaining ingredients, cover and cook slowly for about $1\frac{1}{2}$ hours. Remove the bayleaf and drain the meat, retaining the liquor. Mince the meat finely and stir in the liquor. Press it into a $1\frac{1}{2}$-pt. dish, cover with foil and cook in the oven at 350°F, 180°C (mark 4) for 30 minutes. Leave in a cold place. When cool, refrigerate.

When required
Turn out the pâté and garnish with lettuce, cucumber and tomato.

Pâté maison

$\frac{1}{2}$ lb. chicken livers
3 oz. lean pork or veal
2 oz. fresh white breadcrumbs
4 fl. oz. milk
salt and pepper
pinch of nutmeg
streaky bacon rashers, cut thinly and rinded
sprig of thyme
1 bayleaf
$\frac{1}{8}$ pt. aspic jelly, made from aspic jelly powder
$\frac{1}{2}$ tbsp. brandy

SERVES 4

1 day ahead
Mince the liver finely once and the pork or veal twice. Soak the breadcrumbs in milk. Season the liver and pork with salt, pepper and nutmeg. Stir in the breadcrumbs gently, otherwise the liver will lose its colour. Line a 1-pt. terrine with very thin slices of streaky bacon, then put in the liver mixture. Top with more bacon and add the thyme and bayleaf. Cover with a lid and place in a roasting tin. Pour water into the tin to a depth of 1 in. Place it in the oven at 325°F, 170°C (mark 3) and cook for about $1\frac{1}{2}$ hours.

Add a little melted aspic jelly and the brandy 15 minutes before the end of cooking time. Remove from the oven.

When the pâté begins to cool, remove the lid and place a plate and a weight on top. Allow it to cool completely before covering with the remaining aspic. Store, covered, in the refrigerator.

When required
Serve with crusty French bread.

Soups make popular starters or a snack meal in themselves.

Potted beef

1 lb. stewing steak, cut into
  ½-in. cubes
¼ pt. stock
1 clove
1 blade of mace
salt and pepper
2 oz. butter, melted
fresh bayleaves for garnish

SERVES 6

1 day ahead
Put the cheese, lemon rind, egg yolks and cream in a small bowl. Place the bowl over a pan of hot water and cook, stirring, until smooth and thick. Remove from the heat. Season with salt, pepper, cayenne pepper and garlic. Chop the smoked salmon finely and add it to the cheese mixture with the chopped parsley and breadcrumbs. Spoon into 6–8 individual soufflé dishes or ramekins until about two-thirds full. Melt the butter and pour a little into the top of each dish. Chill.

When required
Serve with thinly sliced brown bread and butter.

Taramasalata

8 oz. fresh smoked cod's roe,
  skinned
12 tbsps. olive oil
2 tbsps. lemon juice
finely grated rind of ½ lemon
1 tsp. grated onion
1 tbsp. chopped parsley
freshly ground black pepper
sprig of parsley for garnish
1 lemon for garnish

SERVES 6

1 day ahead
Put the roe and 6 tbsps. olive oil in a bowl and leave for 15 minutes. Pass it through a fine sieve or blend in an electric blender until smooth, gradually adding the lemon juice and the remaining 6 tbsps. oil.

If the blender has been used, turn the roe into a bowl, and then stir in the lemon rind, onion, chopped parsley and pepper to taste. Chill in a serving dish.

When required
Garnish with a sprig of parsley. Serve with plump wedges of lemon for squeezing, and with fingers of hot crisp toast.

Thrifty pâté

1¼ lb. lean belly pork
½ lb. pig's or ox liver
¼ lb. lean streaky bacon,
  rinded
4 oz. onion, skinned and
  chopped
1 small clove garlic, skinned
1 level tsp. salt
freshly ground black pepper
1 oz. butter

SERVES 6

1–2 days ahead
Remove the rind and any bones from the belly pork and dice it. Rinse the liver under cold running water and dry on absorbent paper. Cut it into largish pieces. Mince the pork, liver, bacon, onion and garlic together three times. Work in the salt and pepper.

Turn the meat into a 2-pt. terrine or small casserole, cover and place it in a small roasting tin with water to come half-way up. Cook at 300°F, 150°C (mark 2) for about 1½ hours. Remove

ERRATUM

We regret that the methods
for the recipes Potted beef and
Potted smoked salmon (pages 66 & 67)
have been transposed.

double sheet of foil over the top, add
l weight down until the pâté is quite
ably in a refrigerator. Remove the
covering, melt the butter over a low
over the pâté and chill.

ired
ast or French bread.

Potted smoked salmon

2 3-oz. pkts. full fat soft
    cheese
finely grated rind of 1 lemon
2 egg yolks
½ pt. double cream
salt and freshly ground black
    pepper
cayenne pepper
1 clove garlic, skinned and
    crushed
6 oz. smoked salmon
    trimmings
4 tbsps. finely chopped parsley
2 oz. fresh white breadcrumbs
2 oz. butter

SERVES 6–8

1 day ahead
Put the meat in a casserole with the stock and
seasonings. Cover and cook in the centre of the
oven at 350°F, 180°C (mark 4) for 2½–3 hours,
until tender. Remove the clove and mace and
drain off the stock, setting it aside.

    Mince the meat twice or place it in a blender
and blend for several minutes until smooth. Add
1 oz. melted butter and sufficient of the reserved
stock to moisten it. Press the meat into ramekins
or soufflé dishes, cover with the remainder of the
melted butter and chill.

When required
Serve garnished with a fresh bayleaf on each
portion.

Kipper pâté

12 oz. kipper fillets
6 tbsps. dry white wine
2 tbsps. lemon juice
4 oz. butter, softened
freshly ground black pepper
6 tomato slices
Melba toast

SERVES 6

1 day ahead
Remove the skin from the kipper fillets. Place
them in a shallow dish and spoon the wine over.
Cover and leave to marinade in a cool place for 4
hours. In a bowl, work the fillets and marinade
to a paste with a wooden spoon, or purée in an
electric blender until smooth, adding the lemon
juice to make a softer mixture.

    Beat in the softened butter and season with
black pepper. Divide between 6 3½-fl.-oz. ramekin
dishes. Smooth over the tops and mark with a
fork. Refrigerate.

1 hour ahead
Remove the pâté from the refrigerator and allow
it to come to room temperature. To serve, top
each with a tomato twist. Serve with Melba toast.

Chilled cucumber soup (*see page 62*)

Smoked haddock ramekins

8 oz. smoked haddock
1 level tbsp. aspic jelly
   crystals
2 tbsps. boiling water
¼ pt. natural yoghurt
8 capers, chopped
2 hard-boiled eggs, chopped
salt and pepper
paprika pepper and parsley
   for garnish

SERVES 6

1 day ahead
Poach the haddock in water until flaking. Drain and skin it and mash until smooth. Dissolve the aspic jelly crystals in the boiling water, then stir in the yoghurt, fish, capers and eggs. Season to taste. Divide the mixture between 6 ramekins. Chill.

1 hour ahead
Remove from the refrigerator. Garnish with a sprinkling of paprika and sprigs of parsley.

Peter's pâté (*see page 63*)

Tunafish creams

$7\frac{1}{2}$ fl. oz. soured cream
2 tbsps. mayonnaise
salt and pepper
dash of Worcestershire sauce
$\frac{1}{2}$ tbsp. chopped chives
2 tsps. capers, chopped
$\frac{1}{2}$ level tsp. finely grated onion
$\frac{1}{4}$ oz. powdered gelatine
2 tbsps. water
7-oz. can tuna steak, drained
  and flaked
2 eggs, hard-boiled and
  chopped
2 firm tomatoes for garnish
parsley

SERVES 4–6

1 day ahead
Combine the soured cream, mayonnaise, seasonings, herbs and onion. Dissolve the gelatine in the water in a basin over a pan of hot water. Cool slightly and stir it into the cream mixture; add the tuna steak and eggs and mix well. Spoon into individual soufflé dishes and refrigerate.

When required
Serve garnished with tomato wedges and parsley.

Potted shrimps

$\frac{3}{4}$ pt. peeled shrimps
6 oz. butter, melted
ground mace
cayenne pepper
ground nutmeg
clarified butter
sliced cucumber and lemon

SERVES 6

1 day ahead
Heat the shrimps very slowly in the butter, without allowing them to come to the boil. Add seasonings to taste, then pour the shrimps into small pots or glasses. Leave them to become quite cold, then pour a little clarified butter over each. Store in the refrigerator.

When required
Turn out the shrimps on to individual plates, retaining the shape of the pots. Garnish with cucumber slices and twists of lemon. Serve with brown bread and butter.

Danish herring salad

3 tbsps. cherry brandy
1 level tbsp. tomato paste
1 level tsp. French mustard
1 tsp. Worcestershire sauce
1 tbsp. malt vinegar
4 whole pickled herrings
1 small onion, skinned and
  quartered
capers and finely chopped
  onion for garnish

SERVES 4

1 day ahead
Whisk together the cherry brandy, tomato paste, mustard, Worcestershire sauce and vinegar. Drain the herrings, slice them thickly and arrange with the onion quarters in a dish. Pour the marinade over the fish to cover. Leave in a cool place.

10 minutes ahead
Arrange the drained herrings in small dishes. Spoon a little of the marinade over and garnish with capers and finely chopped onion.

Marinaded mushrooms

1½ lb. button mushrooms
juice of 1 large lemon
12 fl. oz. wine vinegar
1 small clove garlic, skinned
2 medium onions, skinned and
  chopped
1 bouquet garni
1 level tsp. salt
freshly ground black pepper
½ pt. olive oil
1½ tbsps. tomato ketchup
chopped parsley, to garnish

SERVES 4

1 day ahead
Wipe the mushrooms. Put them in a pan with the lemon juice and enough water to cover and bring to the boil. Boil for 5 minutes then leave until cold.

Meanwhile, put the wine vinegar into a saucepan and add the garlic, chopped onion, bouquet garni, salt and pepper. Bring to the boil and boil, uncovered, for 5 minutes. Remove the garlic and cool the liquor. Add the olive oil and tomato ketchup.

Drain the mushrooms well and put into a deep bowl. Pour the dressing over and leave to marinade overnight, in the refrigerator.

1 hour ahead
Remove the mushrooms from the refrigerator. To serve, lift out the mushrooms, place in a shallow dish, sprinkle with the chopped parsley, and pour over them the dressing, strained through a sieve.

Mushrooms à la grecque

1 onion, skinned and finely
  chopped
4 tbsps. olive oil
¼ pt. dry white wine
bouquet garni
1 clove garlic, skinned
salt and black pepper
1 lb. button mushrooms
½ lb. tomatoes, skinned and
  halved
chopped parsley

SERVES 6

1 day ahead
Sauté the onion in 2 tbsps. oil until soft. Add the wine, bouquet garni, garlic and seasoning. Wipe the mushrooms and seed the tomatoes. Add them to the onion mixture and cook gently, uncovered, for about 10 minutes. Remove from the heat and cool. Remove the bouquet garni and garlic and add the remaining oil if required. Chill.

Just before serving
Sprinkle with chopped parsley.

Tomato appetisers

3 oz. piece Parmesan cheese
12 firm red tomatoes
salt and freshly ground black
  pepper
dried basil
¼ pt. single or double cream

SERVES 6

1 day ahead
Grate the cheese and store it in the refrigerator in a plastic bag.

1 hour ahead
Peel the tomatoes and cut in half. Arrange 4 halves in each of 6 individual soufflé dishes with Parmesan, salt and pepper. Sprinkle with more cheese and a dusting of basil. Spoon cream over the top. Place the dishes on a baking sheet.

Potted shrimps *(see page 70)*

Above right: Mushrooms à la grecque *(see page 71)*

Right: Danish herring salad *(see page 70)*

20 minutes ahead
Cook towards the top of the oven at 375°F, 190°C (mark 5) for about 15 minutes. Serve hot.

Tomato jelly rings

1 lb. firm ripe tomatoes
2 small onions, skinned and
   chopped
1 small clove garlic, skinned
   and crushed
1 level tsp. sugar
$\frac{1}{2}$ level tsp. salt
pinch of celery salt
pinch of grated nutmeg
1 bayleaf
1 tsp. peppercorns
1 level tbsp. powdered gelatine
1 tbsp. tarragon vinegar
3 tbsps. lemon juice
watercress for garnish

SERVES 4

1 day ahead
Scald the tomatoes, remove the skins, cut them in quarters and remove the centres if tough. Put the tomatoes, onions, garlic, sugar, salts and nutmeg in a pan, add the bayleaf and peppercorns tied in muslin and cook over a low heat until the onion is tender. Remove the muslin bag. Dissolve the gelatine in 2 tbsps. water in a small basin over hot water. Work the tomato mixture in an electric blender, rub it through a sieve, and turn it into a measure. Add the vinegar and lemon juice and if necessary make up to 1 pt. with water. Add the dissolved gelatine, pour into wetted individual ring moulds and leave to set in the refrigerator.

When required
Turn out the moulds and garnish with watercress.

Courgettes à la grecque

2 small onions, skinned and
   thinly sliced
3 tbsps. olive oil
1 clove garlic, skinned and
   crushed
$\frac{1}{4}$ pt. dry white wine
salt and pepper
$1\frac{1}{4}$ lb. courgettes
1 lb. tomatoes, peeled,
   quartered and seeded
fresh chervil for garnish

SERVES 4

1 day ahead
Sauté the onions in the oil until soft but not coloured. Add the garlic, wine and seasoning. Wipe the courgettes and discard the end slices. Cut the remainder into rings. Add the courgettes and prepared tomatoes to the pan and cook gently without covering for 10 minutes. Cool. Store, covered, in a cool place.

When required
Garnish with chervil.

Avocado and melon cocktail

2 charentais (or 1 cantaloup)
   melons
$\frac{1}{4}$ watermelon, optional
4 avocados
lemon juice
fresh mint, to garnish

SERVES 4

1–2 hours ahead
Cut the charentais (or cantaloup) melons in half and discard the seeds. Scoop out as much of the flesh as is practical with a small vegetable baller and retain the skins. Cut open the watermelon and cut out the flesh in the same way. Keep all the melon balls in a cool place.

As near as possible to serving time
Cut the avocados in half lengthwise, remove the stones and scoop out the flesh with the same size baller. Sprinkle the avocado balls with lemon juice to prevent discoloration. Pile the melon and avocado balls into the charentais melon skins and top with a sprig of mint. If cantaloup melons are used one half will serve 2 people. Chill for up to 30 minutes before serving.

Ham and pineapple cocktail

6 oz. sliced ham
1 slice pineapple
2 tbsps. double cream,
  whipped
$\frac{1}{2}$ tbsp. tomato ketchup
juice of $\frac{1}{4}$ lemon
shredded lettuce
paprika pepper to garnish

SERVES 4

1 day ahead
Remove any fat from the ham and cut the ham into matchstick-size pieces. Shred the pineapple. Stir together the cream, ketchup and lemon juice. Store the ham, pineapple and dressing separately in the refrigerator, in covered containers.

10 minutes ahead
Toss together the ham, pineapple and dressing. Arrange a little shredded lettuce in the base of individual glasses. Spoon the ham mixture on top. Garnish with a light dusting of paprika.

Tomato jelly rings *(see page 74)*

Ham and pineapple cocktail *(see page 75)*

Avocado and melon cocktail *(see page 74)*

5. Salads and Vegetables

Make the most of salads and vegetables to simplify meal preparation. The majority of them can be prepared in advance and kept in polythene bags in the refrigerator, or a cool place, to keep fresh and crisp, and then assembled when they're needed. Dressings, too, can be made in advance (see 'In Store' chapter). Jellied salads can be made well ahead, so they are particularly useful for parties.

When you're preparing a green salad, divide the greenery into bite-size pieces with your hands, and then toss it gently so as not to bruise, using just enough dressing to make the leaves glisten – not to make them soggy. Don't dress green salads until just before eating. But more robust salads such as potato mayonnaise, cloeslaw, raw mushroom salad, can be prepared and left to marinade in the dressing overnight.

Generally speaking, partial cooking of vegetables beforehand isn't a good idea, and is also unnecessary, since cooking time is comparatively short. Most vegetables – with the exception of potatoes – are often better for being a little undercooked. But the preparation, which does take time, can be carried out beforehand.

When it comes to serving vegetables, even the plainest can be dressed up with a sprinkling of chopped herbs; try parsley on carrots, mint on peas, and tarragon on courgettes. Grated nutmeg also goes well with carrots.

The servings given in this section are for side salads and accompanying vegetables.

Rice salad

8 oz. long grain rice
4 oz. French beans
4 oz. frozen peas
8 oz. tomatoes
2 oz. chopped celery (when available)
2 oz. chopped apple
½ tbsp. chopped parsley
½ tbsp. chopped chives
French dressing (well flavoured with mustard)
2 bunches cress

SERVES 8

Up to 5 days ahead
Cook the rice, rinse and drain thoroughly and allow to cool. When quite cold, cover tightly and place in the refrigerator.

1 day ahead
Cook the beans and peas. Scald the tomatoes and skin them; quarter and remove the seeds; strain the juice and reserve it. Keep the beans, peas, tomato quarters and juice in separate lidded containers in the refrigerator.

2 hours ahead
Turn the rice into a bowl; add the beans, celery, peas and apple. Stir lightly with a fork, adding the parsley, chives, tomato juice and enough dressing to moisten. Pile in the centre of a dish, arranging the tomatoes round the sides and the cress at each end.

Pasta salad

4 oz. macaroni
salt
chopped chives
French dressing

SERVES 4

1 day ahead
Cook the macaroni in boiling salted water until tender. Drain thoroughly and allow it to cool, then cut into 1 in. lengths. Cover and keep in a cool place.

2 hours ahead
Add chopped chives and toss gently in French dressing.

Potato salad

1–1½ lb. potatoes
1 level tbsp. finely chopped onion (optional)
¼ pt. mayonnaise
1 tbsp. chopped parsley or mint

SERVES 4

1 day ahead
Boil the potatoes in their jackets. Peel and slice or dice, then add the chopped onion. When cold, mix with sufficient mayonnaise to moisten. Cover and keep in the refrigerator.

Just before serving
Sprinkle with parsley or mint.

Note: New or waxy potatoes give the best results. (You can leave tiny new potatoes whole.) Potatoes dressed while hot will need more mayonnaise.

Variations
Rub the salad bowl with cut garlic and omit the onion.

Fold in chopped celery heart, cucumber cubes, grated carrot or celery seeds before serving.
Add chopped red pepper to the parsley for an attractive garnish.

Mushroom salad

1 lb. open mushrooms
3 tbsps. lemon juice or cider vinegar
¼ pt. salad oil
3 tbsps. finely chopped parsley
freshly ground black pepper
salt

SERVES 4–6

1 day ahead
Wash and dry the mushrooms, if necessary. Do not peel. Remove the stalks and slice the caps very thinly into a serving dish. Add lemon juice, oil, parsley and pepper and marinade in the dressing. Keep, covered, in refrigerator.

Just before serving
Lightly season with salt and serve with fish.

Jellied beetroot and apple salad

1-pt. red jelly tablet
½ pt. boiling water
¼ pt. vinegar
2 tbsps. lemon juice
1 lb. cooked beetroot
2 eating apples
2 oz. shelled walnuts

SERVES 4–6

1 day ahead
Break up the jelly tablet, place it in a basin and dissolve it in the boiling water. When it is dissolved, mix together the vinegar and the lemon juice, make up to ½ pt. with cold water and add to the hot jelly liquid. Peel and slice or dice the cooked beetroot; peel, core and slice the apples. Place the walnuts in the base of a 2-pt. ring mould and add the beetroot and apple in layers. Pour on the liquid jelly and leave in the refrigerator.

When required
Unmould on to a flat plate and garnish.

Red cabbage and sweetcorn salad

1 medium-sized red cabbage
⅛ pt. French dressing
11-oz. can sweetcorn kernels
½ cucumber, diced
salt and freshly ground black pepper
¼ level tsp. finely grated lemon rind
½ tbsp. clear honey

SERVES 6

1 day ahead
Quarter the cabbage, discard the coarse stems and shred the cabbage very finely. Store in a plastic bag in a cool place.

About 2½ hours ahead
Place the cabbage in a large bowl with the dressing. Toss and leave for 2 hours. Drain the corn. Place the cucumber, seasoned with salt and pepper, in a bowl; leave for 2 hours.

30 minutes ahead
Drain off any excess moisture from the cucumber

The quickest side dish for any meal is a salad of seasonal vegetables

and add with the corn, lemon rind and honey to the cabbage. Toss thoroughly.

Continental cucumber

1 cucumber
2 level tsps. salt
2 tbsps. water
3 tbsps. salad oil
2 tbsps. wine or tarragon
vinegar
2 level tsps. sugar

SERVES 4–6

1 day ahead
Wipe the cucumber, discard the ends and slice the middle thinly. Sprinkle with salt. Cover with a plate and weight down for 30 minutes. Toss the slices on kitchen paper to drain. Mix together the water, oil, vinegar and sugar. Place the cucumber in a bowl and sprinkle with dressing. Store, covered, in the refrigerator.

Moulded cucumber and carrot ring

1-pt. lemon jelly tablet
$\frac{1}{4}$ pt. water
$\frac{1}{4}$ pt. cider vinegar
$\frac{1}{4}$ pt. white wine
4 oz. carrot, coarsely grated
6 oz. cucumber, cut into small dice

SERVES 4

1 day ahead
In a saucepan, gently melt the jelly in the water. Remove from the heat and add the vinegar and white wine. Chill the jelly until it is the consistency of unbeaten egg white. Combine the vegetables and fold them through the setting jelly. Pour it into a $1\frac{1}{4}$-pt. capacity plain ring mould. Chill until firm.

When required
Unmould in the usual way.

Avocado and tomato salad

$\frac{1}{2}$ medium green pepper
2 tomatoes
1 small onion
1 avocado
juice of $\frac{1}{2}$ lemon
snipped parsley

For the dressing
4 tbsps. salad oil
2 tbsps. wine vinegar
$\frac{1}{2}$ level tsp. caster sugar
$\frac{1}{4}$ level tsp. salt
$\frac{1}{4}$ level tsp. dry mustard
$\frac{1}{4}$ level tsp. Dijon mustard
freshly ground black pepper

SERVES 4

1 day ahead
Seed and very thinly slice the pepper. Skin and slice the tomatoes. Skin the onion and cut it into paper-thin rings. Refrigerate these ingredients in separate containers. Shake together all the dressing ingredients.

15 minutes ahead
Halve, stone, peel, and slice the avocado; squeeze a little lemon juice over. Arrange the pepper, tomatoes, onion and avocado on four small plates. Moisten with dressing and garnish with snipped parsley.

This goes well with steaks, grilled cutlets, and sausages, too.

Pineapple and pepper salad

28-oz. can pineapple pieces
1 green pepper
$\frac{1}{4}$ cucumber (or $\frac{1}{2}$ a small ridge
   cucumber)
1 lettuce
2 oz. sultanas
4 tbsps. French dressing

SERVES 6

1 day ahead
Drain the pineapple and reserve the juice. Seed, blanch and slice the pepper. Keep it in a plastic bag in a cool place.

A few hours ahead
Dice the cucumber, wash and shred the lettuce.

10 minutes ahead
Mix the pineapple, pepper, cucumber, sultanas and lettuce. Combine the French dressing with 2 tbsps. pineapple juice, pour it over the salad and toss well.

Tomato coleslaw

1 lb. white cabbage
3 oz. seedless raisins
$\frac{1}{2}$ pt. thick mayonnaise
salt and freshly ground black
   pepper
1 lb. crisp green eating apples
juice of 1 lemon
1 lb. tomatoes

SERVES 6–8

A few hours ahead
Shred the cabbage finely. In a large bowl, combine it with the raisins and mayonnaise. Season well.

Just before serving
Wipe the apples, core and dice; leave the skins on. Place in a basin with the lemon juice and toss lightly to coat evenly with juice. Add to the cabbage mixture. Place $\frac{2}{3}$ of the mixture in a deep serving dish, levelling the surface. Slice the tomatoes crosswise, season, and place half in a layer over the slaw. Cover with remaining cabbage mixture, making a cone shape in the centre. Arrange a circle of overlapping tomatoes around the top edge. Keep in a cool place.

South Seas tomato salad

$\frac{3}{4}$ lb. tomatoes, peeled and
   quartered
4 tbsps. French dressing
$15\frac{1}{2}$-oz. can pineapple rings,
   drained
4 oz. green pepper, seeded

SERVES 4–6

A few hours ahead
Remove the seeds from the tomato quarters (scoop them out with a teaspoon – they can be used for sauces, stews, casseroles, etc.). Marinade the quarters in French dressing. Reserve $1\frac{1}{2}$ slices pineapple for garnish; chop the remainder. Dice the pepper. Keep pepper and pineapple in separate containers in a cool place.

10 minutes ahead
Add the pepper and pineapple to the tomato quarters; toss lightly in the dressing. Pile into a dish, garnish with the reserved pineapple and some of the tomato quarters.

Leek salad

2 leeks
3 tomatoes
2 tsps. chopped parsley
a little freshly chopped basil,
   optional
$\frac{1}{4}$ pt. garlic French dressing

SERVES 4

1 hour ahead
Remove two-thirds of the green from the leeks.
Slice the leeks finely and wash in cold water;
drain. Peel the tomatoes, halve, and discard the
seeds; chop the flesh and add this with parsley
and basil to the dressing. Pour over leeks.

Confetti salad

1 large cucumber
1 lb. firm tomatoes, skinned
   and halved
$\frac{1}{2}$ lb. young carrots, scraped
small bunch radishes,
   trimmed
celery seed dressing (see
   method)

SERVES 6

A few hours ahead
Cut the unpeeled cucumber in $\frac{1}{4}$-in. slices and
then cut each slice into sticks. Remove the seeds
from the tomatoes and cut the flesh into strips.
Slice the carrots in rings and cut into sticks as for
the cucumber. Combine these ingredients in a
large bowl. Make up a French dressing, using
lemon juice instead of vinegar, and flavour with
celery seeds.

Just before serving
Add enough dressing to moisten the vegetables.

Leek and tomato salad

4 young tender leeks, washed
4 small tomatoes, skinned
1 lettuce
1 level tsp. chopped fresh basil
1 level tsp. chopped fresh
   chervil
3 tbsps. French dressing

SERVES 4

A few hours ahead
Slice the white part of the leeks very finely. Cut
the tomatoes into sections. Wash and drain the
lettuce. Put the vegetables into a dish and sprinkle
on the basil and chervil.

Just before serving
Pour the dressing over the salad.

Creamed spinach

$\frac{1}{2}$ lb. uncooked spinach per
person

SERVE WITH GRILLS

1 day ahead
Wash the spinach well in several waters to remove
all grit, and strip off any coarse stalks. Chop
roughly. Pack it into a saucepan with only the
water that clings to the leaves after washing.

   Heat gently, turning the spinach occasionally,
then bring to the boil and cook gently until soft,
about 10–15 minutes. Drain thoroughly. Push
through a nylon sieve or purée in a blender. Cool
and keep, covered, in the refrigerator.

Buy vegetables in season—it's cheapest and there is always a
variety available

Add 1–2 tbsps. cream and some salt and pepper. Reheat gently in a saucepan.

Aubergine au gratin

1 lb. aubergines

salt and freshly ground black pepper

butter

8 oz. tomatoes, skinned and sliced

1–1½ oz. Parmesan cheese, grated

¼ pt. single cream

2 oz. fresh white breadcrumbs

SERVES 4

1 day ahead
Wipe aubergines and cut into ½-in. slices. Sprinkle seasoning over. Butter a 3-pt. ovenproof casserole. Place a third of the aubergines in the base. Cover with some of the tomatoes. Sprinkle a thin layer of cheese over; dot with butter before repeating with aubergine, tomato, seasoning and butter, finishing with a layer of aubergine. Pour the cream over. Combine the breadcrumbs and the rest of the cheese together and sprinkle evenly over the aubergine. Store, covered, in a cool place.

About 1¼ hours ahead
Bake, covered, in the oven at 350°F, 180°C (mark 4). If necessary, remove lid after 1 hour and turn temperature up to 400°F, 200°C (mark 6) for 15 minutes to brown the topping.

Glazed new carrots

1 lb. young carrots, scraped and left whole

2 level tbsps. brown sugar

juice of 1 orange

knob of butter

chopped parsley

SERVES 4

1 day ahead
Simmer the carrots in salted water for about 15 minutes, or until cooked. Drain. Cool. Keep covered.

10 minutes ahead
Mix the cooked carrots with the sugar, orange juice and butter; heat gently in a pan to melt the butter, then simmer for 5 minutes. Serve sprinkled with parsley.

Carrot ring

2½ lb. new carrots

1 oz. butter

¼ pt. chicken stock

1 level tbsp. caster sugar

½ level tsp. salt

freshly ground black pepper

2 oz. Canadian Cheddar cheese

1 large egg, beaten

6 oz. shelled peas

SERVES 4

1 day ahead
Scrape and trim the carrots; cut into short lengths. Place them in a large saucepan with the next 5 ingredients. Cover and cook until the carrots are tender and the liquid has been absorbed. Mash the carrots well until smooth. Grate the cheese and add to the carrots. Adjust seasoning. Beat the egg and fold it into the carrot mixture. Refrigerate, covered.

1 hour ahead
Transfer the mixture into a 1½-pt. aluminium ring

mould. Place it on a baking sheet and reheat in the oven at 350°F, 180°C (mark 4) for 45 minutes. Invert the ring on to a warmed plate; unmould and fill the centre with freshly cooked peas.

Green beans with almonds

1 oz. blanched almonds
2 oz. butter
1½ lb. French beans, topped
   and tailed
salt
freshly ground black pepper

SERVES 6

1 day ahead
Cut the almonds into thin strips, with a small pointed knife. (It helps to pour boiling water over and to soak them a few minutes to soften them. Drain and then slice.) Melt 1 oz. butter in a frying pan. Add nuts and fry until golden brown. Keep on one side.

20 minutes ahead
Cook the beans in boiling salted water until tender – about 15 minutes. Drain and toss with remaining butter, seasoning and almonds.

Red cabbage and apple

1 medium sized red cabbage
¾ pt. salted water
4 cooking apples, peeled, cored
   and sliced
pinch of ground nutmeg
2 oz. butter
1 level tbsp. sugar

SERVES 4

1 day ahead
Wash and finely shred the cabbage. Boil the salted water and add the cabbage, apples and nutmeg. Simmer gently until the cabbage is cooked and most of the liquid has evaporated. Allow to cool. Store, covered, in a cool place.

5 minutes ahead
Reheat quickly. Add the butter and sugar just before serving. (A good accompaniment to sausages, especially Frankfurters.)

Baked tomatoes

2 oz. long grain rice
8 large, firm tomatoes
1 oz. butter
2 oz. frozen peas, cooked
salt and pepper

SERVES 4–6

1 day ahead
Cook the rice and drain. Cut a thin slice from the rounded end of each tomato; scoop out a little of the seed and core. Store tomatoes and rice in a cool place, covered.

20 minutes ahead
Put a knob of butter on each tomato and bake in the oven at 350°F, 180°C (mark 4) for about 10 minutes. Meanwhile, reheat the rice (see page 142). Cook the peas, drain. Season the rice, spoon it into the tomatoes and top with peas.

Celery with tomatoes

1 head celery – about ¾ lb.
1 lb. firm red tomatoes
1 oz. butter
pinch of dried tarragon
freshly ground pepper

SERVES 4

1 day ahead
Trim the celery and wash it thoroughly; scrub the stems if necessary. Slice it thickly. Cook in boiling salted water until tender – about 20 minutes. Drain thoroughly. Skin and quarter the tomatoes. Keep the celery and tomatoes in a cool place.

10 minutes ahead
Melt 1 oz. butter in a saucepan and add the tarragon, then the cooked celery and tomato quarters. Cover and cook over a slow heat for about 5 minutes. Shake the pan occasionally. Add coarsely ground pepper.

Cauliflower niçoise

1 small onion
½ lb. firm tomatoes
1 oz. butter
1 small clove garlic, skinned and crushed
freshly ground black pepper
1 medium cauliflower
salt
1 tbsp. chopped parsley

SERVES 4

1 day ahead
Niçoise mixture: Remove the onion skin and slice the flesh finely. Peel the tomatoes, halve them and discard the pips. Cut the flesh into squares. Melt the butter and fry the onion until soft. Lightly stir in the tomato and crushed garlic. Heat through; season with black pepper. Cool and store, covered, in a cool place.

20 minutes ahead
Divide the cauliflower head into florets and cook these in boiling salted water for about 10 minutes. Drain the cauliflower thoroughly and keep it warm.

5 minutes ahead
Reheat the niçoise mixture gently in a frying pan. To serve, arrange the cauliflower in a dish; top with the tomato mixture and plenty of parsley.

Buttered cucumber

1 large plump cucumber
water
salt
knob of butter
freshly ground black pepper

SERVES 6

A few hours ahead
Thinly pare the skin from the cucumber, using a potato peeler. Cut the cucumber into about 2-in. lengths and each piece into 4, lengthwise; remove some of the seed area. Place the cucumber in a saucepan with just enough water barely to cover, add salt and cook for about 7 minutes; make sure the cucumber stays crisp. Drain off the liquid and keep the cucumber in a cool place.

Just before serving
Melt the butter in a pan with the pepper. Heat the

cucumber through gently, shaking carefully. Serve with lamb.

Ratatouille

2 onions, skinned and sliced
2 red or green peppers, seeded and sliced
2 tbsps. olive oil
4 courgettes, trimmed and sliced
1 aubergine, peeled and diced
2 shallots, skinned and chopped (optional)
2 tomatoes, skinned and roughly chopped
salt and pepper
chopped parsley

SERVES 4

1 day ahead
Fry the onions and peppers lightly in the olive oil. Add the courgettes and aubergine, mix well, then add the shallots, tomatoes and plenty of seasoning. Cover and cook on a low heat for 30 minutes, until the vegetables are soft and the volume slightly reduced. Cool and store covered in the refrigerator.

1 hour ahead
Reheat, if wished, in a covered casserole in the oven at 350°F, 180°C (mark 4) or in a pan on top of the cooker and sprinkle with chopped parsley. Or serve cold.

Petits pois à la française

$\frac{1}{4}$ of a lettuce, washed and finely shredded
6 spring onions, halved and trimmed
a little parsley and mint, tied together
$1\frac{1}{2}$ lb. shelled peas
$\frac{1}{4}$ pt. water
1 oz. butter
salt and pepper
2 level tsps. sugar
butter for serving

SERVES 4–6

A few hours ahead
Put all the ingredients except the extra butter in a pan, cover closely and simmer until cooked – about 20–30 minutes. Remove the parsley and mint and drain the peas well, reserving the liquid. Keep in an airtight container in a cool place.

A few minutes ahead
Heat the liquid and the peas through gently; drain the peas again when heated and serve with a knob of butter.

French-style potatoes

2 lb. potatoes, peeled
2 level tbsps. Dijon mustard
2 level tbsps. chopped chives
$\frac{1}{2}$ pt. milk or stock
salt and freshly ground black pepper
1 oz. butter, melted

SERVES 6

1 day ahead
Slice the potatoes thickly and layer half in an ovenproof casserole. Combine the mustard, chives, stock and seasonings and pour half over the potatoes. Add another layer of potatoes and pour the remaining stock over. Brush melted butter over the surface of the potatoes. Season with salt and pepper. Cover and keep in a cold place.

2 hours ahead
Cook, covered, in the oven set at 350°F, 180°C (mark 4).

Duchesse potatoes

1 lb. potatoes, boiled and
   drained
2 oz. butter
1 egg
salt and pepper
grated nutmeg

SERVES 4

1 day ahead
Sieve or mash the potatoes, add the butter, egg, and seasoning, and beat well until the mixture is very smooth. Pipe into rosettes on a greased baking sheet. Keep in a cool place.

30 minutes ahead
Bake near the top of the oven at 400°F, 200°C (mark 6) until golden brown.

Potato croquettes

1 lb. potatoes, boiled and
   drained
1 oz. butter
1 egg, beaten
1 tsp. chopped parsley
salt and pepper
egg and browned crumbs for
   coating
fat for deep frying

SERVES 4

1 day ahead
Sieve or mash the potatoes and add the butter, egg, parsley and seasoning. Form the mixture into small balls or rolls and coat with egg and crumbs – twice if possible, as this helps to prevent breaking. Keep covered in a cool place.

10 minutes ahead
Heat the fat until a 1-in. cube of bread takes 40–50 seconds to brown. Fry the croquettes for 4–5 minutes, drain well and serve immediately.

Anna potatoes

1½ lb. even-sized waxy
   potatoes, peeled
salt and pepper
melted butter

SERVES 4

1 day ahead
Peel and slice the potatoes thinly, trimming them to give equal-sized slices. Keep in cold water.

2 hours ahead
Grease a thick cake tin and line the bottom with greased greaseproof paper. Dry the potatoes thoroughly, using a teatowel. Arrange a layer of slightly overlapping slices in the tin. Sprinkle with salt, pepper and melted butter.

Continue in this way until all the potatoes have been used, pressing each layer well into the tin. Cover with greaseproof paper and a lid and bake for about 1 hour in the centre of the oven at 375°F, 190°C (mark 5). Add more butter if the potatoes begin to look dry. Turn out and serve at once.

Gingerbread

8oz   self raising flour
1 level tsp Baking powder
¼ "   "   Bicarbonate of Soda
1½ "   "   ginger

} all sieved

2 tbsp golden syrup
3oz margarine or butter
4oz soft brown sugar

} all melted

Add ¼ pint of milk and 1 beaten egg
Mix together and bake for an hour at
Gas 4
180°

Scones (Nane's)

1 lb	Plain Flour .
1 Tspn	Soda Bi Carb.
2 "	Cream of Tarter .
	Pinch of Salt .
4 oy	Sugar
	Saltanas
4 oy	Veg Oil .
2	Eggs .
1 Tea cup	of milk .

Put all dry ingredients into a mixing bowl. Add the Veg Oil and rub in very well, beat eggs, and add to miss with milk .

Roll out lightly and cut, bake in a hot oven 450° for 10 min or until brown

Pan sauté potatoes with chives

2 lb. small new potatoes
1 oz. butter
1 tbsp. corn oil
salt and pepper
snipped chives

SERVES 6

1 day ahead
Boil the potatoes. Drain and keep, covered, in a cool place.

20 minutes ahead
Melt the butter and oil in a frying pan; when hot, add potatoes and sauté, turning them frequently until the potatoes start to brown. Put in a serving dish and keep hot. To serve, season and garnish with snipped chives.

6. Desserts

In addition to pies (which can be served hot or cold), flans – sponge and pastry – and ice-creams, there are lots of desserts that can be made in advance. Panic-free preparation a few days ahead enables you to produce some exciting looking (and tasting) sweets in next to no time when they're needed. One way you can do this is to have some home-made chocolate or ginger cups or meringue cases at the ready.

Your refrigerator is an invaluable cook-ahead ally; many desserts can be chilled or set and forgotten about until they have to be served – with just a little decoration. Simple desserts are often as acceptable as the more elaborate ones; vanilla ice cream served with one of the sauces given in Chapter 7 will always find a welcome.

If you have a freezer or three-star marked refrigerator you can make ice creams up to 3 months ahead. If your refrigerator has a one or two star marking, consult the manufacturer's instructions. Take ice cream from the freezer and put it in the refrigerator for $\frac{1}{2}$ hour before serving.

Flan pastry

5 oz. plain flour
3 oz. butter or margarine and lard, mixed
$1\frac{1}{2}$ level tsps. caster sugar
1 egg, beaten
4 tsps. water

(This is slightly richer than shortcrust but made in the same way. It is usually sweetened, and ideal for flan cases, tartlets and other sweet pastries.)
Sift the flour and salt together into a bowl and rub in the fat with the fingertips, as for shortcrust pastry, until the mixture resembles fine bread-crumbs. Mix in the sugar. Add the egg and water, stirring until the ingredients begin to bind, then with one hand collect the mixture together and knead very lightly to give a firm, smooth dough.

A fruit pie is an ideal cook ahead recipe—serve hot or cold

To store the dough, wrap it in polythene and keep in the refrigerator, then roll out as for shortcrust pastry and use as required. This quantity of pastry will line a 7–8-in. flan ring.

Flan pastry should be cooked in a fairly hot oven – 400°F, 200°C (mark 6). Cooked flan cases can be stored for several days in an airtight tin.

BAKING BLIND

To bake flans and tarts blind – when they are eventually to be filled with a cold or soft uncooked filling (as with a lemon meringue pie), line the pie dish or flan ring with the pastry. Cut out a round of greased greaseproof paper slightly larger than the pastry case and fit this, greased side down, inside the pastry. Half fill the paper with un-cooked haricot beans or rice or with stale bread crusts. Bake the pastry as directed in the recipe for 10–15 minutes, until it has set. Remove the paper and beans, rice or crusts from the pastry case and return it to the oven for another 5 minutes or so to dry out. It is now ready to use.

Alternatively, line the pastry case with kitchen foil, which does not need filling with beans.

Sponge flan cases

2 eggs
2 oz. caster sugar
2 oz. plain flour

Grease an 8½-in. sponge flan tin. Place a round of greased greaseproof paper on the raised part of the tin to prevent sticking. Put the eggs and sugar in a large bowl, stand it over hot water and whisk until the mixture is light and creamy and thick enough to show a trail when the whisk is lifted. Remove from the heat and whisk until cool.

Sift half the flour over the whisked mixture and fold in very lightly, using a tablespoon. Add the remaining flour in the same way. Pour the mixture into the flan tin, spread it evenly with a palette knife and bake above the centre of the oven at 425°F, 220°C (mark 7) for about 15 minutes. Loosen the edge carefully, turn the flan case out on to a wire rack and leave to cool.

Flan fillings

Raspberry cheese

3 oz. cream cheese
1 tbsp. milk
$\frac{1}{2}$ pt. boiling water
$\frac{1}{2}$ 1-pt. raspberry jelly tablet
8 oz. raspberries, fresh or
    frozen
double cream for decoration

SERVES 4

Beat the cream cheese and milk together until smooth. Spread over the base of the flan case. Pour boiling water over the jelly and stir until dissolved. Add the raspberries and stir. When jelly is beginning to set, pour it into the pastry case and leave to set. Just before serving, top with whipped cream.

Fresh fruit

$\frac{1}{2}$ lb. (approx.) fresh fruit, e.g.
    strawberries, raspberries
redcurrant jelly or $\frac{1}{2}$ a 1-pt.
    tablet of red jelly

Pick over the fruit, wash it if necessary and arrange it in the flan case. Make a glaze by melting 2–3 level tbsps. redcurrant jelly with about 1 tbsp. water, or by making up the half-tablet of jelly. Pour the glaze over the fruit when it begins to thicken.

Canned fruit

15-oz. can fruit
3 level tsps. cornflour

Drain the fruit and reserve $\frac{1}{4}$ pt. juice. Arrange the fruit in the flan case, filling it well. Blend the cornflour with a little of the juice to a smooth cream. Heat the rest and stir it into the blended cornflour. Return this mixture to the pan, and bring to the boil, stirring until a clear thickened glaze is obtained. Spoon over the fruit to coat it evenly.

Cinnamon cherry flan

8 oz. flan pastry (8 oz. flour,
    etc.)
1-pt. pkt. vanilla blancmange
1 pt. milk
2 level tbsps. sugar
14-oz. can cherry pie fruit
    filling
$\frac{1}{4}$ pt. double cream and
    cinnamon to decorate

SERVES 4–6

1–2 days ahead
Make an $8\frac{3}{4}$–9-in. fluted pastry case. Roll out the trimmings and with a fluted cutter stamp out 8 leaves; mark veins with a knife, brush them with milk and bake blind alongside the flan case. When cool store in an airtight tin.

A few hours ahead
Make up the blancmange with the milk and sugar. Cool, stirring it occasionally. Spoon into the pastry case. When the blancmange is completely cold, spoon the pie filling over.

1 hour ahead
Lightly whip the cream until it just holds its shape. Pipe 12 whirls round the edge of the flan. Place a pastry leaf on each alternate whirl and dust the remaining whirls with cinnamon.

Solve all your problems by serving fresh fruit as a dessert

Cherry and almond pie

12 oz. shortcrust pastry (12 oz.
   flour, etc.)
raspberry jam
2 oz. ground almonds
2 oz. caster sugar
1 large egg, beaten
$\frac{3}{4}$ lb. cherries, stoned
caster sugar for dredging

SERVES 4–6

1 day ahead
Make the pastry.

A few hours ahead
Roll out the pastry and use half to line a 7-in. pie plate. Spread raspberry jam over the base. Blend together the ground almonds, sugar and egg and spread half this mixture over the jam. Add the cherries and cover with the remaining almond mixture. Cover the pie with a lid made from the remaining pastry and seal the edges. Decorate with leaves cut from the pastry trimmings.

Bake in the oven at 375°F, 190°C (mark 5) for 30–40 minutes. Cool and dredge with caster sugar.

Lemon shorties

10 oz. plain flour
4 oz. caster sugar
6 oz. butter, softened
2 egg yolks

For filling
1 oz. butter
½ pt. single cream
1 oz. plain flour
2 oz. caster sugar
2 egg yolks
grated rind ½ lemon
½ tsp. vanilla essence
icing sugar

MAKES ABOUT 12

1 day ahead
Make the pastry; sift the flour on to a working surface, make a well in the centre and place in the sugar, butter and egg yolks. Use the finger tips of one hand and work the flour into the other ingredients. Knead lightly. Refrigerate for about 15 minutes. Roll out the pastry on a floured surface. Cut 12 rounds with a 3-in. plain cutter and 12 rounds with a 2½-in. fluted cutter. Line 12 deep patty tins with plain rounds.

A few hours ahead
Make the filling; heat the butter and half the cream in a small pan. Blend the flour and sugar and add the remaining cream. Add this gradually to the mixture in the pan, beating well until smooth. Remove from the heat and beat in the egg yolks, lemon rind and essence. Return to the heat and cook gently for 5 minutes. Allow to cool. Divide the filling between the pastry cases. Place the fluted lids in position, press down lightly.

Bake at 400°F, 200°C (mark 6) for 15–18 minutes until lightly browned. Allow to cool in the tin before turning out. Serve dusted with icing sugar.

Basic genoese sponge
(for gâteaux)

1½ oz. butter
2½ oz. plain flour
½ oz. cornflour
3 large eggs
3 oz. caster sugar

Grease and line a 9-in. straight-sided sandwich tin or a 7-in. square cake tin. Heat the butter gently until it is melted, remove it from the heat, and let it stand for a few minutes. Sift together the flour and cornflour. Place the eggs in a large deep basin over a saucepan of hot water, whisk for a few seconds, add the sugar and continue whisking over the heat until the mixture is very pale in colour and a trail forms when the whisk is lifted. Remove it from the heat and whisk for a few seconds longer. Re-sift half the flour over the egg and carefully fold it in, using a metal spoon. Then pour in the melted butter (cooled until it just flows) round the side, folding it in alternately with the remaining flour. Turn the mixture into the prepared tin and bake near the top of the oven at 375°F, 190°C (mark 5) for about 30 minutes, or until well risen and just firm to the touch. Turn out carefully and leave to cool on a wire rack.

Raspberry shortcake gâteau

10 oz. plain flour
2 oz. ground rice
8 oz. butter
4 oz. caster sugar
finely grated rind of 1 lemon
2 oz. shelled walnuts, finely
  chopped
1 egg yolk
$\frac{1}{2}$ pt. double cream
2 $15\frac{1}{2}$-oz. cans raspberries or
  loganberries, well drained,
  or $1\frac{1}{2}$ lb. fresh fruit

SERVES 8

Several days ahead

Place the flour, ground rice, butter, sugar, and lemon rind in a bowl and rub in until the mixture resembles fine breadcrumbs. Add the walnuts and egg yolk and knead together to give a soft dough. Wrap in a polythene bag and chill for 30 minutes. Roll two-thirds of the dough into a rectangle 12 in. by 6 in. and place it carefully on a baking sheet. Roll out the remainder, cut six 3-in. rounds with a pastry cutter and cut each in half. Place these on a baking sheet. Bake at 350°F, 180°C (mark 4) allowing about 30 minutes for the rectangle and about 20 minutes for the semicircles, until light brown and firm. While the pastry is still warm on the baking sheet, cut the rectangle in half lengthwise with a sharp knife. Cool. Wrap in foil to store.

About an hour ahead

Whip the cream until stiff and, with a large rose vegetable nozzle, pipe two-thirds of the cream in a thick line down the centre of one shortbread. Spoon most of the fruit over the cream, put the second piece of shortbread on top, press down lightly and pipe the remaining cream in whirls down the centre. Arrange the semicircles along the cream and put a whole berry between each.

Velvet refrigerator cake

24–26 soft sponge fingers
6 oz. caster sugar
2 level tbsps. cornflour
$\frac{3}{4}$ pt. milk
$\frac{1}{2}$ pt. double cream
2 oz. unsweetened chocolate
2 egg yolks
1 oz. butter
1 level tsp. powdered gelatine
2 tsps. water
toasted flaked almonds for
  decoration

SERVES 4–6

1 day ahead

Line a loaf tin 7 in. by 5 in. by $2\frac{1}{2}$ in. with a strip of non-stick paper. Arrange some sponge fingers to cover the base and sides. In a saucepan, blend together the sugar and cornflour and gradually stir in the milk and $\frac{1}{4}$ pt. cream. Break the chocolate into pieces, add it to the milk and bring slowly to the boil, stirring all the time. Boil gently for 2–3 minutes, still stirring. Cool for a few minutes and then beat in the egg yolks. Return it to the heat and cook for 1 minute. Beat in the butter.

Sprinkle the gelatine over 2 tsps. water; stir it into the chocolate mixture when dissolved. Cool, stirring occasionally. When the mixture is beginning to thicken, pour half of it over the sponge fingers. Cover with another layer of sponge fingers and spoon over the remaining chocolate mixture; cut the fingers level with the chocolate mixture and use the bits to place over the chocolate in a final layer. Leave overnight in the refrigerator.

1 hour ahead
Turn out the cake on to a flat dish. Whip the rest of the cream. Cover the top of the cake with this cream and sprinkle with almonds.

Orange cheesecake

3 oranges
juice of 1 lemon
2 level tbsps. powdered
  gelatine
2 eggs, separated
$\frac{1}{2}$ pt. milk
3 oz. caster sugar
1 lb. 4 oz. plain cottage cheese
$\frac{1}{4}$ pt. double cream, whipped
extra whipped cream for
  decoration

For crumb base
4 oz. digestive biscuits
2 oz. caster sugar
2 oz. butter, melted

For decoration
3 oranges, peeled and
  segmented

SERVES 6–8

1 day ahead
Finely grate the rind of 2 oranges, squeeze the juice from 3, and add the lemon juice. Put 4 tbsps. of the mixed juices in a small bowl and sprinkle the gelatine over. Whisk together the egg yolks, milk and 2 oz. sugar. Turn into a pan and cook, without boiling, for a few minutes. Add the soaked gelatine and stir continuously until dissolved. Leave to cool until just starting to set, then add the grated orange rind and 6 more tbsps. mixed juices.

Sieve the cheese and beat it into the jelly mixture – or blend in a blender. Whisk the egg whites stiffly, add 1 oz. sugar and whisk again until stiff. Fold quickly into the almost set cheese mixture, followed by the whipped cream. Turn the mixture into a 3-pt. ($9\frac{1}{2}$-in.) deep sloping sided cake tin, its base lined with non-stick paper. Crush the biscuits and stir in the sugar and butter. Spread this over the cheese mixture and press lightly with a round-bladed knife. Store in the refrigerator.

About an hour ahead
Turn out the cheesecake and decorate with overlapping segments of orange and whirls of double cream. Return it to the refrigerator until required.

Chocolate cups

8 oz. plain chocolate

For filling
1-pt. pkt. lime jelly
8 tbsps. sherry
4 tbsps. orange juice
2 tbsps. apricot jam, sieved
8 oz. sponge cake crumbs
2 tbsps. milk
$\frac{1}{4}$ pt. double cream

MAKES 16

Several days ahead
Melt the chocolate in a bowl standing over warm water. Set out some paper bun cases, using two together for firmness; carefully and evenly coat the inside of each with melted chocolate. Allow to harden in a cool place; re-coat if necessary. These can be made well in advance, providing they are stored in airtight containers in a cold place.

1 day ahead
Make up the jelly as directed on the packet. Pour half of it into a shallow tin and leave in a

Raspberry shortcake gâteau *(see page 98)*

cool place to set. Blend together the sherry, orange juice and jam and stir in the sponge cake crumbs. Carefully ease the paper cases from the shells and divide the cake crumb mixture between the chocolate cups. Whisk the half-set jelly in a measure until frothy, and divide between the cups. Whisk the milk and cream together until the mixture will hold its shape, and pipe it round the edge of each cup. Dice the remaining jelly and spoon it into the centre of the cream ring. Keep in the refrigerator until required.

Ginger cups

2 oz. butter
2 oz. caster sugar
2 level tbsps. golden syrup
2 oz. plain flour
½ level tsp. ground ginger
1 tsp. brandy
grated rind ½ lemon

For filling
½ pt. double or whipping
   cream
2 oz. stem ginger, chopped
stem ginger for decoration

MAKES 12

Several days ahead
Make the cups. Melt the butter with the sugar and golden syrup. Off the heat, beat in the flour, ginger, brandy and lemon rind. Cool for about 2 minutes. Place 3 or 4 tsps. of the mixture, well apart, on baking sheets lined with non-stick parchment paper. Bake in rotation towards the top of the oven for 7–10 minutes, until deep golden brown. Remove from the oven.

As the mixture becomes firm, lift with a palette knife and drape each one over the base of a buttered 1-lb. jam pot. When set, remove and store in an airtight tin.

1 hour ahead
Make the filling by whipping the cream and folding in chopped ginger. Divide it between the ginger cups and decorate each with a slice of ginger.

Meringue shells

6 large egg whites
12 oz. caster sugar

MAKES 12

Line 2 baking trays with non-stick paper. Whisk the egg whites until stiff, then whisk in half the sugar until the mixture becomes stiff again. Fold in the remaining sugar. Spoon the meringue into 12 heaps on the prepared baking trays, keeping them well apart. Make into flan shapes, hollowing out the centres with the back of a spoon. Dry out the shells in the oven at the lowest setting for about 2½–3 hours. Peel off the paper and cool the shells on a wire rack. Store in an airtight tin.

Note: If you prefer, mark 3-in. circles on the paper and spread some of the meringue mixture over to form the base of the shells. Then, with a large star vegetable nozzle, pipe the remainder to form the edge.

Filling for meringue shells

Ginger cream

½ pt. double cream
¼ pt. single cream
6 tbsps. finely chopped stem ginger

FILLS 12 SHELLS

Whip the creams lightly together and fold in half the chopped ginger. Divide the ginger cream between the meringue shells and top with the remaining chopped ginger.

Other ideas for fillings
Fresh fruit mixed with whipped sweetened cream.
Canned fruit glazed with jam.
Pie filling, liquer-flavoured and topped with a cream swirl.
Fresh fruit and ice cream.

Pineapple meringue torte

1-lb. 4-oz. can pineapple chunks
4 egg whites
8 oz. caster sugar
pinch cream of tartar
4 oz. blanched almonds, finely chopped

For filling
½ pt. double cream
3 tbsps. milk
icing sugar

1 day ahead
Turn the contents from the can of pineapple into a saucepan and boil until the juice is reduced almost entirely and the pineapple looks opaque. Cool. Whisk the egg whites in a deep bowl until stiff, add 2 tbsps. of the measured sugar and cream of tartar and whisk again until stiff. Fold in the remainder of the sugar and the finely chopped nuts. Spread in two 8–9-in. discs over non-stick baking paper placed on baking sheets. Dry in the oven at 300°F, 150°C (mark 2) for about 1¼ hours until the almond meringue is crisp and the paper peels away easily. Cool and store in an airtight tin or in kitchen foil.

A few hours ahead
Whip the cream and milk together until thick enough to spread. Use about two-thirds to sandwich the meringue discs together, along with most of the pineapple. Place the meringue on a serving plate and dust with icing sugar. Using a fabric forcing bag and a medium vegetable rose nozzle, pipe whirls of cream round the top edge of the torte. Finish with the reserved pineapple and leave to stand in a cool place – preferably the refrigerator – to make the final cutting easier.

Strawberry Pavlova

4 egg whites
8 oz. caster sugar
1 tsp. vanilla essence
1 tsp. vinegar
2 level tsps. cornflour
½ pt. double cream
¼ pt. single cream
1 lb. small strawberries, hulled

SERVES 6

1–2 days ahead
Draw an 8-in. circle on non-stick paper and place on a baking sheet. Whisk the egg whites until stiff and standing in peaks. Continue whisking, gradually adding the sugar, until very stiff. Beat in the vanilla, vinegar and cornflour. Spread the mixture over the circle. Bake just below the oven centre at 300°F, 150°C (mark 1–2) for about 1 hour. Leave to cool. Turn upside down on to a flat serving plate and remove the paper. Store in an airtight tin.

A few hours ahead
Whip the creams until they just hold shape; pile layers of cream and sliced strawberries on to the Pavlova and decorate with strawberry halves. Leave in a cool place – up to 4 hours.

Syllabub

thinly pared rind of 1 lemon
4 tbsps. lemon juice
6 tbsps. white wine or sherry
2 tbsps. brandy
2–3 oz. caster sugar
½ pt. double cream
grated nutmeg or chopped nuts

SERVES 4

1 day ahead
Place the lemon rind, juice, wine and brandy in a bowl and leave for several hours or overnight. Strain into a large bowl, add the sugar, and stir until dissolved. Add the cream slowly, stirring all the time. Whisk until the mixture forms soft peaks. Spoon into glasses and sprinkle with nutmeg or nuts. Store in a cool place – not the refrigerator. Serve with sponge fingers.

Lemon delight

2 whole eggs
2 egg yolks
2 oz. caster sugar
1-pt. lemon jelly tablet
juice and grated rind of 1 lemon
¼ pt. white wine
whipped cream and grated chocolate for decoration (optional)

SERVES 4

1 day ahead
Put the whole eggs, yolks and sugar in a deep bowl over hot, not boiling, water and whisk until really thick. Then allow to cool, whisking occasionally. In a small pan, dissolve the jelly in ¼ pt. water over a very low heat, stirring. Pour it into a measure, add the lemon juice, rind and wine, then make up to 1 pt. with water. Cool until it is on the point of setting, then whisk into the cool egg mixture. Turn into a serving dish and chill.

30 minutes ahead
Decorate if wished with lightly whipped cream and coarsely grated chocolate.

Choc au rhum (*see page 107*)

Grape bavarois

1½ 1-pt. lemon jelly tablets
1 tbsp. lemon juice
hot water
½ lb. white grapes
½ pt. milk
6 level tsps. custard powder
4 level tsps. sugar
½ pt. double cream
black and white grapes for
    decoration

SERVES 6

1 day ahead
Place half a lemon jelly tablet in a graduated measure; add lemon juice and make up to ½ pt. with hot water. When the jelly has dissolved, leave it in a cold place until it is the consistency of unbeaten egg white. Fold in the skinned and pipped grapes and turn it into a 2-pt. ring jelly mould. Leave to set.

Make a custard using the milk, custard powder and sugar. Leave to cool, stirring occasionally to prevent a skin forming. Dissolve the 1-pt. jelly tablet in ⅓ pt. hot water. Leave to set to the consistency of egg white. Whip the cream to the consistency of cold custard and fold it through the custard. Whisk the jelly and fold it into the cream mixture. Spoon this over the set jelly in the mould. Leave in the refrigerator.

1 hour ahead
Unmould on to a serving dish and decorate with sugar-frosted grapes.

Frosted grapes

Using black or white grapes, wash and dry them in threes, pairs or singly. Brush evenly with egg white, then dip in caster sugar to coat. Leave to dry thoroughly overnight.

Crème caramel

For the caramel
2 tbsps. cold water
5 oz. caster sugar
3 tbsps. boiling water

For the custard
1 pt. milk
1 vanilla pod
4 large eggs
2 egg yolks
1½ oz. caster sugar

SERVES 8

1–2 days ahead
Pour the cold water into a small, thick-based frying pan. Stir in the sugar, using a wooden spoon. Place over a low heat to dissolve the sugar, stirring occasionally. When the sugar has dissolved, bring it to the boil and boil without stirring until the sugar turns a dark, golden brown. Remove at once from the heat and slowly spoon in the boiling water, stirring to loosen the caramel. Lightly oil eight ¼-pt. capacity dariole moulds. Spoon some of the caramel into each mould and leave in a cool place until set.

Meanwhile, make the custard. Pour the milk into a saucepan, add the vanilla pod and bring slowly to the boil. Leave to infuse for about 10 minutes. Crack the 4 eggs into a deep bowl and add the extra egg yolks. Add the caster sugar and whisk with a rotary whisk until well blended and pale in colour.

Remove the vanilla pod from the milk, rinse and dry it and store in a jar of caster sugar for further use. Pour the milk on to the eggs, stirring, and strain it into a measuring jug. Skim off the froth from the top, or leave it to subside.

Divide the custard between the caramel-based moulds. Place them in a large roasting tin, in $\frac{1}{2}$ in. cold water. Cover with a double sheet of kitchen foil to prevent a skin forming on the surface of the custards. Cook in the centre of the oven at 325°F, 170°C (mark 3) for about 45 minutes until set. (To test whether the custards are cooked, insert a fine skewer two-thirds of the way through each one; if it comes out clean the custard is cooked.) Remove the moulds from the water and keep in a cool place, or refrigerator.

When required
Ease the custard away from the side of the mould with a small, sharp knife. Shake once and invert into an individual glass dish. Ease the mould away.

Choc au rhum

6 oz. chocolate dots
3 large eggs, separated
1 tbsp. rum
$\frac{1}{4}$ pt. double cream
grated chocolate

SERVES 6

1 day ahead
Melt the chocolate in a bowl over a pan of hot water. Beat the yolks into the melted chocolate with the rum. Whisk the egg whites until stiff and fold evenly into the chocolate mixture. Chill well in individual dishes or glasses. Serve topped with whipped cream and a little grated chocolate.

Crème marron

2 egg whites
$\frac{1}{2}$ pt. double cream
4 level tbsps. sweetened
   chestnut purée
1 tbsp. coffee liqueur
marrons glacés
extra whipped cream, for
   decoration
ratafias

SERVES 4–6

A few hours ahead
Whisk the egg whites until stiff. Whisk the cream until it holds its shape. Mix together the chestnut purée, liqueur and 1 oz. chopped marrons glacés. Fold these into the cream – reserving a little for decoration – with the egg whites. Pile into glasses and refrigerate.

1 hour ahead
Decorate with stars of piped cream, topped with ratafias. Arrange half a marron in the centre of each.

Blackcurrant cream

14-oz. can blackcurrants in
  heavy syrup
2 level tsps. powdered
  gelatine
2 tbsps. water
$\frac{1}{4}$ pt. double cream
$2\frac{1}{2}$-oz. pkt. meringue shells,
  roughly broken

SERVES 4

1 day ahead

Purée the blackcurrants in an electric blender and then put them through a fine sieve to remove any seeds. Dissolve the gelatine in the water in a small basin or cup placed in a pan of hot water. Add a spoonful of the purée to the gelatine, stir and return to the rest of the purée, stirring. Chill until the mixture is just beginning to set. Whisk the cream until it holds its shape and fold it into the purée a little at a time. Fold in the crushed meringues, saving 4 tbsps. for decoration. Spoon the blackcurrant cream into four tall glasses. Chill.

30 minutes ahead

Sprinkle on the remaining meringue.

Fresh stewed sweetened blackcurrants can be used when they are in season; allow about $\frac{3}{4}$ pt. purée.

Apple and orange Bristol

$6\frac{3}{4}$ oz. caster sugar
$\frac{1}{2}$ pt. water
6 dessert or cooking apples,
  peeled and cored
3 oranges
$\frac{1}{2}$ pt. double cream, whipped

SERVES 6

1 day ahead

Make the caramel topping. Put 2 oz. of the caster sugar in a thick pan and heat gently until it becomes a light brown colour, taking care not to let it burn. Pour on to a greased tray, spreading it as thinly as possible, and leave to set. When cold, crush with a rolling pin. Keep this in a cool dry place until the next day.

Put the water and remaining sugar in a thick frying pan, dissolve and bring it to the boil. Quarter the apples and put them into the boiling syrup. Cover and poach gently until just tender. Then leave them to stand in the syrup until they become transparent.

Pare 5–6 very fine strips of rind free of white pith from one of the oranges, cut it into fine shreds and put them in cold water. Bring to the boil and cook for 5–10 minutes, until tender, then drain and dip into cold water. Put these aside until the next day.

Peel the oranges and divide them into segments, free of membrane. Arrange the apple and orange in a dish and pour a little of the syrup over them. Cover and keep in the refrigerator.

When required

Sprinkle the apple and orange with the strips of

Crème marron (see page 107)

orange rind and the broken caramel. Serve with whipped cream.

Pineapple and grape salads

2 medium-sized ripe pine-
    apples
8-oz. can pineapple rings
8 oz. white grapes, halved,
    peeled and pipped
2 oz. trifle sponge cakes
2 tbsps. Kirsch
3 tbsps. lemon juice
2 level tbsps. caster sugar

SERVES 6

1 day ahead
Cut away the top and bottom of each pineapple. Slice each in 3 crosswise. Scoop out almost all the flesh from the 'cases', leaving a 'base' intact. Stand each 'case' on a small plate. Cut the pineapple flesh into small pieces. Drain the canned pineapple, reserving the juice. Shred it and add to the fresh pineapple. Combine with the grapes.

Crush the sponge and divide between the pineapple cases. Mix 6 tbsps. reserved pineapple juice with the Kirsch and spoon it over the sponge.

Heat the remaining juice in a small saucepan with the lemon juice and sugar. Bring it to the boil and continue to boil until a syrup is formed. Remove from the heat and set aside to cool. Fill the pineapple cases with the prepared fruit and keep covered in the refrigerator.

Just before serving
Spoon the syrup over.

Melon and grapefruit jelly

4 level tsps. powdered gelatine
1-lb. 3-oz. can sweetened
    grapefruit juice
2¾ lb. ripe honeydew melon,
    peeled
1 oz. stem ginger

SERVES 6

1 day ahead
Dissolve the gelatine in a little grapefruit juice in a small basin over a pan of hot water, then stir it into the rest of the juice. Stir in the roughly chopped melon flesh and finely chopped ginger. When the jelly is beginning to set, pour it into a 2-pt. mould. Chill to set.

When required
Unmould on to a flat plate for serving.

Oranges à la turque

4 large juicy oranges
½ lb. caster sugar
¼ pt. water
1 clove

SERVES 4

1 day ahead
Thinly pare the rind from two of the oranges free of white pith; cut it into very thin strips with a sharp knife or scissors. Put it into a small pan, cover well with water and cook until the peel is tender; strain.

Cut away all the white pith from the oranges and the rind and pith from the remaining two. Hold the oranges over a bowl to catch the juice and slice carefully into rounds. Reassemble each orange and secure with cocktail sticks.

Dissolve the sugar in the $\frac{1}{4}$ pt. water with the clove. Bring it to the boil and boil until caramel-coloured. Remove from the heat, add 3 tbsps. water, return to a very low heat to dissolve the caramel and add the juice from the oranges. Arrange the oranges in a serving dish, top with the shredded rind, remove the clove and pour the caramel over. Leave in the refrigerator, turning occasionally.

1 hour ahead
Remove from the refrigerator to allow the oranges to come to room temperature.

Pineapple choco crunch

2 oz. butter
4 oz. plain chocolate
2 oz. golden syrup
2 oz. cornflakes
1 oz. walnut halves, chopped
8-oz. can pineapple pieces, drained
$\frac{1}{4}$ pt. double cream
4 walnut halves and grated chocolate for decoration

SERVES 4

1 day ahead
Place the butter, chocolate and syrup in a saucepan and heat gently until smooth. Stir in the cornflakes, walnuts and pineapple. Turn the mixture into a 7-in. sandwich tin and press down well. Refrigerate.

30 minutes ahead
Whip the cream lightly. Turn out the choco crunch carefully on to a flat serving plate, spread evenly with whipped cream and decorate with walnuts and grated chocolate. Serve in wedges.

Apple and blackberry compote

$2\frac{1}{2}$ lb. eating apples
$\frac{1}{2}$ lemon
3 oz. sugar
$\frac{3}{4}$ lb. blackberries
2 tbsps. Calvados liqueur
$\frac{1}{2}$ pt. double cream, lightly whipped

SERVES 6

1 day ahead
Peel, core and thick slice the apples. Poach them in $\frac{3}{4}$ pt. water with a sliver of lemon rind until transparent – about 7 minutes. Drain the apples and set aside to cool. Add the sugar to the cooking liquid, and reduce by half by boiling rapidly in an open pan for about 8–10 minutes. Pour it over the apples.

Place half the apples in the base of 6 individual dishes and cover with half the blackberries. Fill up with layers of remaining apples and berries.

Oranges à la turque *(see page 110)*

Strawberry liqueur ice cream *(see page 115)*

Add the Calvados to the remaining juice and spoon it over the fruit. Refrigerate.

When required
Serve with thick pouring cream.

Lemon freeze

2 oz. cornflakes, crumbled
5 level tbsps. caster sugar
1 oz. butter, melted
2 eggs, separated
small can of sweetened
    condensed milk
4 tbsps. lemon juice

SERVES 8

Up to 2 months ahead
Blend together the cornflake crumbs, 2 tbsps. sugar and the butter until well mixed. Press all but 4 tbsps. into the base of a polythene container suitable for the freezer or frozen food compartment of your refrigerator. Beat the egg yolks in a deep bowl until really thick and creamy. Combine them with the condensed milk. Add the lemon juice and stir until thickened. Beat the egg whites until stiff but not dry, gradually beat in the remaining sugar and fold through the lemon mixture. Spoon this into the polythene tray and sprinkle with the remaining cornflake crumbs. Freeze.

Apricot sherbert

2 eggs, separated
1 oz. caster sugar
16-oz. can apricots, puréed
pinch of ground nutmeg
4 tbsps. single cream

SERVES 4

3–4 hours ahead
Beat the egg whites until stiff and continue whisking while gradually adding half the sugar. Fold in the remaining sugar. Mix the puréed fruit, egg yolks, nutmeg and cream. Fold carefully into the egg whites, then pour immediately into a polythene container and freeze.

When required
Spoon the sherbert into glasses. It should not be too firm.

Fruit ice cream

small can evaporated milk
8 oz. fresh raspberries or a
    15-oz. can, drained, or other
    fruit such as strawberries,
    pears, bananas
2 oz. sugar (if fresh fruit is
    used)

SERVES 4

Up to 3 months ahead
Place the unopened can of milk in a pan of boiling water and keep on the boil for 15 minutes. Remove from the pan, cool and chill thoroughly for several hours. Sieve the fruit to make $\frac{1}{4}$ pt. purée; add the sugar if required. Open the can of milk and whip until stiff. Fold in the purée. Pour it into a polythene container and freeze.

Strawberry liqueur ice cream

$\frac{1}{4}$ pt. double cream, lightly
   whipped
8 oz. strawberries, puréed
$\frac{1}{2}$ tsp. vanilla essence
1 tbsp. rum or maraschino
2 oz. sugar

SERVES 4

Up to 3 months ahead
Mix the cream with all the other ingredients, pour it into a polythene container and freeze for $\frac{3}{4}$–1 hour. Turn out and whisk until smooth. Return the mixture to the container and freeze until firm.

Orange ice cream

$\frac{1}{2}$ pt. double cream
$\frac{1}{2}$ pt. orange juice
caster sugar
mandarin orange sections
wafers

SERVES 4

Up to 3 months ahead
Whip the cream until it holds its shape. Stir in $\frac{1}{4}$ pt. orange juice and add the remaining $\frac{1}{4}$ pt. a little at a time. Add sufficient sugar to make the mixture taste slightly over-sweet. Pour it into a polythene container and freeze.

When required
Serve with mandarin sections and wafers.

Orange sorbet cups

6–7 large oranges (see method)
6 oz. sugar
$\frac{3}{4}$ pt. water
3 tbsps. lemon juice
3 egg whites

SERVES 6

1 day ahead
Using a small, sharp, pointed knife, cut the tops off 6 oranges with a zigzag pattern and scoop out the flesh and membrane. Work over a bowl to catch all the juice. Discard the membrane. Wash the empty shells and put them, with their lids, into the icemaking compartment of the refrigerator or in the freezer.

Dissolve the sugar in the water over gentle heat, bring to the boil, and boil for 5 minutes. Leave to cool.

Purée the orange pulp in a blender or sieve, and make up to $\frac{3}{4}$ pt. with juice from the extra orange, if necessary. Combine the syrup and lemon juice, pour it into a polythene container and freeze until firm – about 1 hour. Whisk the egg whites until stiff but not dry. Turn the frozen fruit mixture into a chilled bowl, break down with a spoon, and fold in the egg whites. Return the sorbet to the container and freeze until firm but still slightly soft in texture.

1 hour ahead
Pack small spoonfuls of orange sorbet into the chilled shells and pile up well. Replace the lids

and chill in the coldest part of the refrigerator –
not the icemaking compartment or freezer.

Rich vanilla ice cream

$\frac{1}{4}$ pt. milk
$1\frac{1}{2}$ oz. sugar
2 egg yolks, beaten
$\frac{1}{2}$–1 tsp. vanilla essence
$\frac{1}{4}$ pt. double cream, partially
   whipped

SERVES 4

Up to 3 months ahead
Heat the milk and sugar and pour them on to the
egg yolks, stirring. Return the mixture to the pan
and cook it over a gentle heat, stirring all the time
until the custard thickens; strain it and add the
vanilla essence. Allow it to cool, fold in the partially
whipped cream, pour into a polythene container
and freeze.

Choc-de-menthe

SERVES 4

Up to 3 months ahead
Make up the basic vanilla ice cream recipe, replacing the vanilla essence by 2 tsps. crème de
menthe and a few drops of green colouring. When
the mixture is half frozen, turn it into a chilled
bowl and whisk. Crumble a small bar of flake
chocolate and fold it in. Return to the container
and freeze.

Orange sorbet cups (*see page 115*)

7. Sauces

Chops, steaks, rissoles, fish fillets and left-overs from the joint benefit from that extra something which a home-made sauce can give. Don't just reach for the bottle on the shelf; try making your own.

If you're making a savoury sauce in advance, you can prevent a skin forming on top if you press a piece of damp greaseproof paper on to the surface; this way it will keep for up to 24 hours if necessary. When needed, re-heat the sauce very gently in a saucepan, or in a double pan or a bowl over a pan of simmering water.

Home-made sauces for ice cream and cold fruit sweets are always welcome; there are several ideas here.

Savoury lemon sauce

rind and juice of 1 lemon
½ pt. white sauce (using half milk and half fish or chicken stock)
1–2 level tsps. sugar
salt and pepper
1–2 tbsps. single cream (optional)

(for grilled fish or chicken)

Simmer the lemon rind in the milk and stock for 5 minutes; strain and use the liquid to make a white sauce (as for Béchamel sauce). When it has thickened, stir in the lemon juice and sugar and season to taste. If the sauce is too sharp, stir in a little single cream just before serving.

Caper sauce

Make some white sauce in the usual way, but use half meat liquor and half milk. Add about 1½ tbsps. coarsely chopped capers to ½ pt. sauce. Serve with boiled lamb or mutton. (Or use half fish liquor for the sauce and serve with poached fish.)

Béchamel sauce

½ pt. milk
1 shallot, skinned and sliced
(or a small piece of onion,
skinned)
a small piece of carrot, peeled
and cut up
½ stick of celery, scrubbed and
cut up
½ bayleaf
3 peppercorns
1 oz. butter
1 oz. flour
salt and pepper

Put the milk, vegetables, bayleaf and peppercorns in a saucepan and bring slowly to the boil. Remove from the heat, cover and leave to infuse for about 15 minutes. Strain the liquid. Melt the butter in a small pan, stir in the flour and cook, still stirring, for 2–3 minutes. Remove the pan from the heat and gradually stir in the flavoured milk. Season to taste and return the pan to a gentle heat. Continue to stir as you bring the sauce to the boil and cook for a further 2–3 minutes.

Tomato sauce

½ onion, skinned and chopped
2 rashers bacon, rinded and
chopped
½ oz. butter
½ oz. flour
15-oz. can tomatoes
1 clove
½ bayleaf
a few sprigs of rosemary (or 1
level tsp. mixed dried herbs)
salt and pepper

(using canned tomatoes)

Fry the onion and bacon in the butter for 5 minutes. Stir in the flour and gradually add the tomatoes, also the flavourings and seasoning. Simmer gently for 15 minutes, then sieve and if necessary re-season.

Serve with croquettes, cutlets, réchauffés, or made-up meat dishes such as beef olives and stuffed peppers.

Devil's sauce

¼ pt. cider vinegar
4 tbsps. Worcestershire sauce
5 tbsps. chilli sauce
½ level tsp. dry mustard
sugar to taste

Mix together the vinegar, sauces and mustard. Cook, stirring occasionally, for about 15 minutes, until reduced and slightly thickened. Add sugar to taste. Serve with grills and barbecues.

Barbecue sauce (1)

8-oz. can tomatoes
2 medium sized onions,
skinned and sliced
1 tbsp. dry cider
½ level tsp. dried or 1 tsp.
chopped fresh basil
salt and pepper
1 clove garlic, skinned and
crushed (optional)

Boil all the ingredients together to reduce the volume, until thick and pulpy. Sieve or blend well; adjust the seasoning. Serve with grilled chops, steaks and barbecues, or with savoury meatballs and patties.

A repertoire of savoury sauces to liven up plain food

To reheat a sauce, put the pan in a water bath and stir until it is heated through

A bolognese sauce can always be cooked a day ahead, for serving with spaghetti (*see page 123*)

Barbecue sauce (2)

2 oz. butter
1 large onion, skinned and chopped
1 level tsp. tomato paste
2 tbsps. vinegar
2 level tbsps. Demerara sugar
2 level tbsps. dry mustard
2 tbsps. Worcestershire sauce
$\frac{1}{4}$ pt. water

Melt the butter and fry the onion for 5 minutes, or until soft. Stir in the tomato paste and continue cooking for a further 3 minutes. Blend the remaining ingredients to a smooth cream and stir in the onion mixture. Return the sauce to the pan and simmer for a further 10 minutes.

Serve with chicken, sausages, hamburgers or chops.

Savoury orange sauce

1 orange
$\frac{1}{2}$ pt. chicken stock
2 level tsps. cornflour
soy sauce

Squeeze the juice from the orange and finely slice half the peel. Add the sliced peel to the stock, bring to the boil and simmer gently until tender; add the orange juice. Mix the cornflour to a smooth paste with 1 tsp. soy sauce and a little water; pour into the orange mixture and return to the boil, stirring until clear. Serve with pork chops.

Quick Creole sauce

¼ pt. tomato juice
1 tsp. Worcestershire sauce
1 bayleaf
1 tbsp. butter
1 level tbsp. flour
1 level tsp. paprika pepper
2 drops Tabasco sauce
¼ level tsp. salt

Simmer the tomato juice, Worcestershire sauce and bayleaf for 5 minutes. Melt the butter, blend in the flour and paprika and cook for 1–2 minutes. Add the tomato mixture, removing the bayleaf. Add the remaining seasonings and re-heat, stirring. Serve with grills.

Mustard sauce

2 oz. margarine
1 oz. flour
1 level tsp. dry mustard
½ pt. water
4 tbsps. vinegar
salt and pepper

Melt the fat, mix in the flour and mustard lightly; add the water gradually, then mix in the vinegar, salt and pepper. Stir and boil gently for 2–3 minutes, until the sauce has thickened. Serve with herrings and made-up fish dishes.

Spicy raisin sauce

3 oz. stoned raisins
2 cloves
½ pt. water
3 oz. brown sugar
1 level tsp. cornflour
salt and pepper
1 oz. butter
2 tsps. lemon juice

SERVES 4

1 day ahead
Put the raisins and cloves in a saucepan with the water, bring to the boil and simmer for about 10 minutes; remove the cloves and add the sugar and cornflour, blended to a cream with a little cold water and seasoned with a pinch of salt and pepper. Stir well as the mixture thickens. Cool and store, covered, in the refrigerator.

When required
Reheat and add the butter and lemon juice. Serve with grilled gammon rashers.

Curry sauce

1 oz. dripping or butter
2 medium sized onions,
    skinned and finely chopped
1 level tbsp. curry powder
1 level tsp. curry paste
1 clove garlic, skinned and
    crushed
⅓ pt. stock or coconut milk
salt
little cayenne pepper
2 level tbsps. chutney
1 tbsp. single cream (optional)

1 day ahead
Melt the fat and fry the onions golden brown, then add the curry powder and paste. Cook for 5 minutes, then add the garlic, pour in the stock or coconut milk and bring to the boil. Add the seasoning and chutney, then simmer for 30–40 minutes.

30 minutes ahead
Add cubes of cold cooked meat to the sauce before reheating. Bring to the boil and heat thoroughly through. Stir in 1 tbsp. cream immediately before serving.

Bolognese sauce

1 onion, skinned and chopped
1 small carrot, peeled and
  chopped
1 stick celery, scrubbed and
  chopped
1 clove garlic, skinned and
  crushed
2 tbsps. olive oil
1 oz. butter
1 bayleaf
$\frac{1}{4}$ pt. Italian red wine
12 oz. raw minced beef
15-oz. can tomatoes
2 level tbsps. tomato paste
meat extract
salt and pepper

SERVES 3

(to serve with pasta)

Up to 3 days ahead
Place the chopped onion, carrot, celery and garlic
in a saucepan with the oil, butter and bayleaf. Fry
for 5 minutes, then add the wine, meat, tomatoes
and tomato paste, with meat extract and seasoning
to taste. Cover and simmer for about 30 minutes.
Adjust seasoning. Cool and store, covered, in the
refrigerator.

When required
Reheat thoroughly in a saucepan. (This amount is
sufficient for accompanying 12 oz. spaghetti;
cook this in boiling salted water for about 20
minutes. Drain, toss in 1 oz. butter and sprinkle
well with black pepper. Place in a hot serving
dish and spoon the sauce over. Serve sprinkled
with Parmesan cheese.)

Savoury Butters

These keep for as long as ordinary butter in the
refrigerator. Either make them into pats or store
as a block and slice the firm butter for serving
with grills and fish.

Lemon butter

1 oz. butter
1 tsp. lemon juice
salt and freshly ground black
  pepper

Cream all the ingredients together and chill
thoroughly.

Maître d'hôtel butter

2 tsps. chopped parsley
squeeze of lemon juice
1 oz. butter
salt
cayenne pepper

Cream all the ingredients together and chill
thoroughly.

Mayonnaise

2 egg yolks
$\frac{1}{2}$ level tsp. dry mustard
$\frac{1}{4}$ level tsp. salt
$\frac{1}{4}$ level tsp. sugar
freshly ground black pepper
$\frac{1}{2}$ pt. salad oil
2 tbsps. lemon juice or 1 tbsp.
    lemon juice and 1 tbsp. wine
    or tarragon vinegar

(Can be kept, covered, for 1–2 weeks in a cool place, preferably a refrigerator.)

Put the egg yolks with the mustard, salt, sugar and pepper in a deep bowl. Mix thoroughly and add the oil drop by drop, holding the basin firmly, and beating with a wooden spoon – or, ideally, use a hand-held mixer, working it round the bowl. When half the oil has been added, beat in 1 tbsp. lemon juice. Beat well. Add the remaining 1 tbsp. lemon juice or vinegar.

Tartare sauce

$\frac{1}{4}$ pt. mayonnaise or salad
    cream
1 tsp. chopped tarragon or
    chives
2 tsps. chopped capers
2 tsps. chopped gherkins
2 tsps. chopped parsley
1 tbsp. lemon juice or
    tarragon vinegar

1 hour ahead
Mix all the ingredients well, then leave the sauce to stand for at least 1 hour before serving, to allow the flavours to blend. Serve with baked, grilled or poached fish.

Rémoulade sauce

2 level tsps. made mustard
1 level tsp. each chopped
    capers and gherkins
1 level tsp. each chopped fresh
    parsley, tarragon and
    chervil
3 fillets of anchovy, chopped,
    or 1 tsp. anchovy essence
$\frac{1}{2}$ pt. mayonnaise

A few hours ahead
Fold all ingredients into the mayonnaise. The sauce should be well flavoured with mustard. It is usually served with grilled meat or fish.

Orange mayonnaise

$\frac{1}{2}$ level tsp. salt
$\frac{1}{2}$ level tsp. dry mustard
pinch white pepper
grated rind 1 orange
2 level tsps. caster sugar
1 egg yolk
$\frac{1}{2}$ pt. vegetable oil
1 tbsp. wine vinegar
1 tbsp. orange juice

1 day ahead
Thoroughly mix the salt, mustard, pepper, orange rind, sugar and egg yolk. Gradually beat in about 3 tbsps. oil. Add the vinegar and beat well. Continue to beat while adding the remaining oil very slowly. Beat in the orange juice.

  This mayonnaise goes very well with a salad served with cold duck, ham, gammon or pork.

Mayonnaise (*see above*)

Green goddess dressing

½ pt. thick mayonnaise
¼ pt. soured cream
3 tbsps. finely chopped parsley
3 tbsps. finely snipped chives
   (or the green tops of spring
   onions)
3 level tbsps. anchovy paste
3 tbsps. tarragon vinegar
1 tbsp. lemon juice
1 clove garlic, skinned and
   crushed
salt and pepper

1 day ahead
Combine all the ingredients in a mixing bowl or electric blender, seasoning to taste. This dressing mellows and thickens on standing. Serve with green, seafood, and chicken salads.

French dressing

1¼ level tsps. salt
freshly ground black pepper
1¼ level tsps. dry mustard
1 level tsp. sugar
¼ pt. tarragon, wine, or cider
   vinegar – or a mixture of
   vinegar and lemon juice
½–¾ pt. salad oil – olive, corn,
   sunflower, etc.

(Make up this larger amount of basic dressing and keep at room temperature for up to 2 weeks, ready to use plain or as a basis for variations.)

Put all the ingredients together in a screwtop jar or plastic-lidded container. Shake vigorously for a few minutes. Use as required, but shake well before adding it to the salad.

French dressing variations

Cheese dressing: Add a little crumbled blue cheese.

Russe dressing: Replace vinegar with lemon juice, add 2 tsps. thin cream and blend well.

Herb dressing: When in season use fresh chopped mint, parsley, chervil, rosemary, etc., with wine vinegar. In winter dried herbs are useful; leave them to marinade in the vinegar an hour or so before required, then blend in the oil just before use.

Pepper dressing: Add a mere touch of chilli or cayenne pepper. Alternatively, add a few drops of chilli sauce.

Crunchy seed dressing: Sprinkle in a few celery, poppy, or caraway seeds.

Brandy butter

3 oz. butter
3 oz. caster or icing sugar
2–3 tbsps. brandy

1 day ahead
Cream the butter until pale and soft. Beat in the sugar gradually and add the brandy a few drops at a time, taking care not to allow the mixture to

Brandy butter is delicious with mince pies and Christmas pudding, and stores like fresh butter (*see above*)

curdle. The finished sauce should be pale and frothy. Pile it up in a small dish and leave in a cool place to harden before serving. Serve with Christmas pudding and mince pies.

Sabayon sauce

2 oz. sugar
4 tbsps. water
2 egg yolks
grated rind of $\frac{1}{2}$ lemon
juice of 1 lemon
2 tbsps. rum or sherry
2 tbsps. single cream

Dissolve the sugar in the water and boil for 2–3 minutes, until syrupy. Pour it on to the beaten yolks and whisk until pale and thick. Add the lemon rind, lemon juice and rum or sherry and whisk for a further few minutes. Fold in the cream and chill well. Serve with cold fruit sweets.

Sauces for Ice Creams and Sundaes

So long as you have ice cream in the refrigerator these sauces will complete a dessert in minutes.

Chocolate sauce

$\frac{1}{4}$ lb. Menier chocolate
small can evaporated milk

Melt the chocolate over a low heat; gradually stir in the evaporated milk and beat well.

Coffee sauce

4 oz. Demerara or granulated
    sugar
2 tbsps. water
$\frac{1}{2}$ pt. strong black coffee

Put the sugar and water in a heavy-based pan and dissolve over a gentle heat, without stirring. Bring to the boil and boil rapidly until the syrup becomes golden in colour. Add the coffee and stir until the 'caramel' has dissolved. Boil for a few minutes, until syrupy. Allow to cool, and serve poured over ice cream.

Melba sauce

4 level tbsps. redcurrant jelly
3 oz. sugar
$\frac{1}{4}$ pt. raspberry purée (from
    $\frac{1}{2}$ lb. raspberries, or a
    15-oz. can)
2 level tsps. arrowroot or
    cornflour
1 tbsp. cold water

Mix the jelly, sugar and raspberry purée and bring to the boil. Blend the arrowroot with the cold water to a smooth cream; stir in a little of the raspberry mixture, and then return the sauce to the pan. Bring to the boil, stirring with a wooden spoon until it thickens and clears. Strain and cool.

Butterscotch sauce

1 oz. butter
1 oz. brown sugar
1 level tbsp. golden syrup
1 oz. nuts, chopped
squeeze of lemon juice
   (optional)

Warm the butter, sugar and syrup until well blended. Boil for 1 minute and stir in the nuts and lemon juice.

Ginger sauce

5 oz. light soft brown sugar
$\frac{1}{2}$ pt. water
3 level tbsps. finely chopped
   stem ginger (about 3 pieces)
$\frac{1}{4}$ level tsp. grated lemon rind

Put all the ingredients in a small pan and dissolve the sugar slowly over a low heat, then bring to the boil and boil for about 8 minutes. When slightly warm, spoon over rich vanilla ice cream. If wished, reheat from cold in a bowl over hot water.

Coffee cream sauce

$\frac{1}{4}$ pt. coffee essence
$\frac{1}{4}$ pt. double cream
1 tbsp. caster sugar
few drops vanilla essence

In a small bowl, whip together the ingredients with a balloon whisk until the cream just begins to hold its shape. Cover and chill in the refrigerator or for up to 24 hours. Stir well before use.

Jam sauce

3 rounded tbsps. jam
a squeeze of lemon juice

Melt the jam over a gentle heat and add the lemon juice.

Fruit purée sauce

canned fruit (black cherries,
   stoned, raspberries and
   strawberries)

Purée the drained canned fruit and spoon over the ice cream in sundae glasses.

Coffee caramel sauce

8 oz. caster sugar
$\frac{1}{2}$ pt. boiling coffee

Dissolve the sugar in a thick pan over moderate heat. Increase the heat to brown the caramel a little. Slowly add the boiling coffee and boil for 6 minutes. Cool slightly, but serve while still warm.

Apricot sauce

Mix some sieved apricot jam with a little lemon juice and 2 tsps. sherry; pour it over ice cream and

Butterscotch sauce *(see page 129);* Melba sauce and Chocolate sauce *(see page 128)*

sprinkle with desiccated coconut or other decoration.

Honey sauce

2 oz. butter
$1\frac{1}{2}$ level tsps. cornflour
4–6 oz. clear honey

Melt the butter in a pan and stir in the cornflour. Gradually add the honey. Bring to the boil and cook for a minute or two.

Marshmallow sauce

4 oz. sugar
3 tbsps. water
8 marshmallows, cut up small
1 egg white
$\frac{1}{2}$ tsp. vanilla essence
red colouring (optional)

Dissolve the sugar in the water and boil for 5 minutes. Add the marshmallows and stir the mixture until they have melted. Whip the egg white stiffly and gradually fold in the marshmallow mixture. Flavour with vanilla, and, if you like, add a drop or two of colouring to tint it pink. Serve at once, over chocolate or coffee ice cream.

Fudge sauce

$\frac{1}{2}$ lb. fudge
6-oz. can evaporated milk
1 level tsp. cornflour
1 tbsp. water
few drops vanilla essence

Heat the fudge and milk together in a small heavy based saucepan until the fudge softens. Blend the cornflour with the water and stir into the fudge and milk with a few drops of vanilla essence. Bring to the boil, stirring. Leave until cold.

Honey and almond sauce

$1\frac{1}{2}$ oz. butter or margarine
1 oz. blanched almonds,
    shredded or flaked
juice of 1 lemon
3 level tbsps. thick honey

Melt the butter or margarine in a saucepan, add the almonds and cook gently until browned. Just before serving, add the lemon juice and honey.

8. In Store

There are lots of things you can make ahead whether or not you need them for a specific occasion. If you have some time to spare, you can soon make a batch of decorations for desserts, or garnishes for savoury dishes, as well as chutneys and other preserves. Surplus bread can be crumbed, dried in a low oven and stored in an airtight container. Likewise if you squeeze an orange for the juice you can grate the rind, dry it and put it away for use later as a cake flavouring. Collect together odd ends of cheese, let them dry out and then grate and store them ready for use with soups and pasta.

These are only a few suggestions. Follow our ideas and you will have a well stocked cupboard ready for all occasions.

Shortcrust pastry

4 oz. plain flour
a pinch of salt
1 oz. lard
1 oz. margarine
4 tsps. water (approx.)

Sift the flour and salt together. Cut the fat into small knobs and add it. Using both hands, rub the fat into the flour between finger and thumb tips. After 2–3 minutes, there will be no lumps of fat left and the mixture will look like fresh bread-crumbs.

(This dry rubbed-in mixture can be kept in the refrigerator for up to a fortnight in an airtight container. Let it 'come to' for a short time, then add water in the usual way.)

When it is needed, add the water a little at a time, stirring with a round-bladed knife until the mixture begins to stick together. With one hand, collect it together and knead lightly for a few seconds, to give a firm, smooth dough. The pastry can be used straightaway, but is better allowed to 'rest' for 15 minutes. It can also be wrapped in polythene and kept in the refrigerator for a day or two.

Note: When a recipe says 8 oz. pastry it means 8 oz. flour plus the fat, etc. If you're using ready-mix and the recipe calls for 4 oz. pastry, measure out 6 oz. and then add the water.

Quantity guide

$\frac{1}{2}$ lb. pastry makes 24 tartlet shells cut with a 3-in. cutter for $2\frac{1}{2}$-in. patty pans $\frac{5}{8}$-in. deep.

$\frac{1}{2}$ lb. pastry makes 24 2-in. sausage rolls.

$\frac{1}{2}$ lb. pastry makes a double crust for an 8-in. pie plate.

$\frac{1}{4}$ lb. pastry makes a simple crust for a 1-pt. pie dish.

$\frac{1}{4}$ lb. pastry makes a 7-in. to 8-in. flan case.

In each instance, increase the quantities slightly if you roll the pastry thicker than $\frac{1}{8}$ in.

Scone mixture can be stored dry in the same way as shortcrust pastry.

Croûtons

Cut slices of white bread $\frac{1}{4}$–$\frac{1}{2}$ in. thick, remove the crusts, then either cut the bread into $\frac{1}{4}$–$\frac{1}{2}$-in. cubes and fry them, or leave the slices whole and grill them before cutting them up. Use as a garnish for soups. Cut into larger triangles and crescents, croûtons can be used as a garnish for minced meat or au gratin dishes.

Croûtons can be stored – when cool – in an airtight container, and refreshed in the oven for a short time when required.

Fleurons

Roll out puff pastry trimmings thinly, and stamp out rounds using a $1\frac{1}{2}$-in. fluted cutter. Brush with beaten egg, fold over into semicircles and place on a baking sheet; glaze the tops with egg and sprinkle poppy seeds over. Leave in a cool place for 30 minutes, then bake in the oven at 400°F, 200°C (mark 6) for about 15 minutes. Serve warm. You can make them ahead and reheat in the oven as required. They add texture and taste as an accompaniment to most soups, seafood casseroles and chicken fricassees.

Keep a variety of commercial flavourings to hand

Beetroot chutney

2 lb. raw beetroot, shredded
   or grated
1 lb. onions, skinned and
   chopped
1 lb. 8 oz. apples, peeled,
   cored and chopped
1 lb. seedless raisins
2 pt. malt vinegar
2 lb. sugar
6 level tsps. ground ginger

MAKES ABOUT 6 lb.

Place all the ingredients in a preserving pan and bring to the boil. Simmer over a moderate heat, uncovered, for about 1 hour until soft and pulpy. Pot and cover with vinegar-proof parchment or lids.

Green tomato chutney

1 lb. apples, peeled and cored
$\frac{1}{2}$ lb. onions, skinned
3 lb. green tomatoes, thinly
   sliced
$\frac{1}{2}$ lb. sultanas
$\frac{1}{2}$ lb. Demerara sugar
$\frac{1}{2}$ oz. salt
$\frac{3}{4}$ pt. malt vinegar
$\frac{1}{2}$ oz. dried whole root ginger
$\frac{1}{2}$ level tsp. cayenne pepper
1 level tsp. dry mustard

MAKES ABOUT 3 lb.

Mince the apples and onions and put them in a pan with the rest of the ingredients. Bring to the boil, reduce the heat and simmer until the ingredients are tender and reduced to a thick consistency, with no excess liquid. Remove the ginger; put into warm jars and cover with vinegar-proof parchment or lids.

Apple and tomato chutney

2 lb. apples, peeled, cored and
   sliced
2 lb. tomatoes, skinned and
   sliced
$\frac{3}{4}$ lb. onions, skinned and
   chopped
1 clove garlic, skinned and
   chopped
$\frac{1}{2}$ lb. mixed dried fruit
$\frac{3}{4}$ lb. Demerara sugar
$\frac{1}{2}$ oz. mustard seed, tied in
   muslin
$\frac{1}{2}$ oz. curry powder
1 level tsp. cayenne pepper
1 oz. salt
$1\frac{1}{2}$ pt. malt vinegar

MAKES ABOUT 5 lb.

Stew the apples in a very small quantity of water until tender. Put the apples, tomatoes, onions and garlic into a pan with the dried fruit, sugar, spices, salt and vinegar. Bring to the boil, reduce the heat and simmer until the consistency is thick and there is no excess liquid. Remove the muslin bag, pour into warm jars and cover with vinegar-proof parchment or lids.

Rhubarb and orange chutney

2 oranges
2½ lb. prepared rhubarb
3 onions, skinned and
   chopped
1½ pt. vinegar
2 lb. Demerara sugar
1 lb. raisins
1 level tbsp. mustard seed
1 level tbsp. peppercorns
1 level tsp. allspice

MAKES ABOUT 8 lb.

Squeeze the juice from the oranges, pare the peel, free of white pith, and shred finely. Place these in a large preserving pan with the rhubarb, onions, vinegar, sugar and raisins. Tie the spices in a piece of muslin and add to the pan. Bring to the boil and simmer until thick and pulpy. Remove the muslin, pour into warm jars, and cover with vinegar-proof parchment or lids.

Tarragon vinegar

Fill a wide-necked jar with tarragon leaves, freshly gathered just before the plant flowers. Fill with wine vinegar, cover with vinegar-proof parchment or a coated lid and leave in a cool dry place for about 6 weeks. Strain through double muslin; taste and add more vinegar if the tarragon flavour is too strong. Pour into bottles and seal with vinegar-proof lids.

Mint preserved in vinegar

To every ½ lb. freshly picked mint leaves, allow 1 lb. sugar and 1 pt. vinegar. Wash and dry the leaves; chop finely and put into dry, wide-necked jars. Dissolve the sugar in the vinegar, stirring with a wooden spoon; allow it to come just to the boil, then remove from the heat. When cold, pour over the chopped mint and seal the jars with vinegar-proof parchment or lids.

To make mint sauce, remove sufficient mint with a wooden spoon, along with a little of the liquid. Mix with a little fresh vinegar.

Herb spice

1 oz. each dried powdered
   bayleaves, thyme,
   marjoram and basil
1½ level tbsps. powdered mace
1½ level tsps. powdered
   nutmeg
1½ level tsps. ground black
   pepper
1½ level tsps. powdered cloves

Mix and sift the herbs and spices together. Put into clean, dry glass jars and label. Use for flavouring meat or sausage dishes, stuffing, etc.

Apple and tomato chutney (*see page 136*)

Nut refrigerator cookies

3 oz. butter or margarine
3 oz. Demerara sugar
1 egg, beaten
6 oz. self-raising flour
3 oz. walnuts or almonds,
   finely chopped

MAKES 24

2–3 days ahead
Cream the butter and sugar and gradually beat in the egg. Stir in the flour and chopped nuts to give a fairly firm dough. Shape into a long roll, wrap in a polythene bag or aluminium foil and put in the refrigerator for several hours – or days – to chill thoroughly.

When required
Cut the roll into $\frac{1}{4}$-in. slices, place the biscuits, widely spaced, on greased baking trays, and bake for 10–12 minutes at 400°F, 200°C (mark 6). Cool on a wire rack.

Dried fruits, nuts and pasta give you last minute trimmings for many
meals. Airtight glass jars make attractive storage containers

Vegetables need cool, airy storage

Rainbow refrigerator cookies

3 oz. butter or margarine
3 oz. caster sugar
1 egg, beaten
6 oz. self-raising flour
pinch of salt
$\frac{1}{4}$ oz. cocoa
grated rind of $\frac{1}{2}$ a lemon
1 oz. glacé cherries, finely
 chopped
cochineal

MAKES 24

Cream the butter and sugar and beat in the egg gradually. Sift the flour with the salt and stir it into the creamed mixture. Divide the dough into three. Stir the cocoa into one portion and roll out on a lightly floured board to an oblong 8 in. by 5 in. Add the lemon rind to the second portion and roll out to the same size. Add the cherries and a few drops of cochineal to the last portion, and roll into a third oblong. (If the mixture is too soft to handle, cover it and chill in a refrigerator or cool place.)

Sandwich the lemon portion between the cocoa and cherry portions and roll up lengthwise like a Swiss roll. Trim the edges, wrap firmly in a polythene bag or aluminium foil and put in the refrigerator for some hours – or several days – to chill until quite firm. To finish, cut the roll into $\frac{1}{4}$-in. slices and place the biscuits, widely spaced, on greased baking trays and bake at 400°F, 200°C (mark 6) for 10–12 minutes. Cool on a wire rack.

Sugar crisps

(for decorating cream toppings)

Use some fairly soft royal icing to pipe 1–1$\frac{1}{2}$-in. diameter discs freehand on to foil-lined baking sheets. Dry for about 1 hour then place under a low grill, still on the foil, for about 10 minutes until completely dried and tinged pale brown. The leaves when ready should slip easily off the foil. Turn them over and dry a little longer. Cool before storing. They'll keep for up to a week in an airtight container.

Praline leaves

Put 5$\frac{1}{2}$ oz. caster sugar in a heavy-based pan and dissolve over a low heat. When it is a deep caramel colour, add 4 oz. nibbed almonds a little at a time, stirring with a metal spoon. Turn quickly on to a clean oiled baking sheet or marble surface and use a whole lemon to roll out the praline thinly. With warm cutters, stamp out oval leaf shapes. If the praline sets too quickly, put it in a warm oven for a few minutes. Crush the trimmings to store for a week or so.

The leaves can be stored for several days if you

put them in an airtight container with non-stick paper between the layers.

Chocolate almonds

(for putting in the centre of a whirl of cream)

Melt a small amount of plain chocolate cake covering. Dip whole or halved blanched almonds in the chocolate to half-coat. Allow the excess to drip off. Leave to set on non-stick paper. Keep in a cool place.

Tuiles d'amandes

2 egg whites
4 oz. caster sugar
2 oz. plain flour
2 oz. flaked or nibbed almonds
2 oz. butter, melted

Whisk the egg whites until stiff and fold in the caster sugar, sifted flour and almonds. Mix well. Fold in the cooled melted butter. Place teaspoonfuls of the mixture well apart on a greased baking sheet. Smooth out each one thinly with the back of a spoon, keeping them round.

Bake for 8–10 minutes at 375°F, 190°C (mark 5) until lightly browned. Use a palette knife to lift each one from the baking sheet and place it over a rolling pin, so that it sets in a curled shape. Allow a moment or two for the wafer to harden and then remove to a wire rack to cool.

Store in an airtight container until needed. Serve with cream desserts, mousses, and other soft-textured sweets.

Coffee syrup

4 oz. Demerara sugar
2 tbsps. water
½ pt. strong black coffee

Dissolve the sugar in the water over a low heat. Boil until the mixture caramelises. Add the coffee, stir until the caramel is dissolved, then boil for a few minutes until the mixture becomes syrupy. This can be stored, when cold, in a screwtop jar for up to 2 weeks. Use with ice cream, for flavouring buttercream and for milk shakes.

Vanilla sugar

is more satisfactory for flavouring sweet dishes than vanilla essence; make your own by keeping a vanilla pod in a jar of caster sugar. Keep covered and use as required.

Melba toast

can be kept in an airtight tin. Traditionally, it is made by toasting $\frac{1}{4}$-in. slices of bread, splitting them through the middle, and then toasting the uncooked surfaces. Or you can cut stale bread into very thin slices and lay them on baking sheets to dry off at the bottom of the oven at 250°F, 130°C (mark $\frac{1}{2}$) until they are crisp and curled. Brown them slightly in a warm oven (325°F, 170°C (mark 3)) or under a very low grill, then allow them to cool before storing.

Buttered crumbs

can be used dry for coating rissoles, or can be tossed with butter or grated cheese for topping other dishes. To make them, melt 1 oz. butter and add 1 pt. fine white breadcrumbs. Let the crumbs absorb the fat, forking the mixture several times. Spread out on baking sheets and dry in the oven on its lowest setting. When ready, they are cream-coloured and dry. Stored in a screwtop jar or polythene bag in a cool place, they will keep fresh for 2 months.

Cooked rice

can be kept in a refrigerator – tightly covered – for up to 5 days, or in a cold larder for 2 days. When required, reheat it by putting it into a pan with a few tablespoonfuls of water, cover, and place over a very low heat. Shake occasionally. Leave for a few minutes until rice is hot and fluffy.

Cooked pasta

(after rinsing until all stickiness disappears, then draining) can be kept, covered, in the refrigerator, for a day. To reheat, freshen it first under hot water and then drain and toss in hot butter.

Seasoned flour

– for flouring meats, poultry and vegetables before

frying, or for preparing meat to be used in casseroles – keeps well. Mix 1 lb. plain flour, 2 oz. salt, $\frac{1}{2}$ oz. pepper, $\frac{1}{2}$ oz. dry mustard and, if you wish, some freshly chopped or dried herbs (such as 2 rounded tsps. each thyme and parsley and 1 rounded tsp. sage or tarragon).

Beurre manié

(for thickening stock or the liquid in a casserole-type dish). Cream equal quantities of butter and flour with a fork to a smooth paste. Add the paste gradually, in pieces, to the hot liquid to give the required thickness and smoothness of texture. After adding and gently blending with a whisk or fork, the liquid should be brought slowly to boiling point, but not boiled hard. Make in advance and keep in a lidded container in the refrigerator.

Refrigerator Storage Times

FOOD	HOW TO STORE	DAYS
Meat, raw		
Joints	Rinse blood away; wipe dry, cover loosely with	3–5
Chops, cut meat	polythene or foil	2–4
Minced meat, offal	Cover as above.	1–2
Sausages	Cover as above.	3
Bacon	Wrap in foil or polythene, or put in plastic container.	7
Meat, cooked		
Joints	In tightly wrapped foil or polythene or in	3–5
Sliced ham	lidded container.	2–3
Continental sausages	As above.	3–5
Casseroles	In lidded container.	2–3
Loaves	In foil or polythene.	2
Poultry, raw		
Whole or joints	Draw, wash, wipe dry. Wrap loosely in polythene or foil.	2–3
Poultry, cooked		
Whole or joints	Remove stuffing; when cool, wrap or cover as for cooked meats.	2–3
Made-up dishes	Cover when cool.	1
Fish, raw (white, oily, smoked)	Cover loosely in foil or polythene.	1–2
Fish, cooked	As above, or in covered container.	2
Shellfish	Eat the day it is bought – don't store.	
Vegetables, salads		
Prepared green and root vegetables, green beans, celery, courgettes, aubergines, peppers	In 'crisper' drawer, or in plastic container, or wrapped in polythene.	5–8
Sweetcorn, mushrooms, tomatoes, radishes, spring onions	Clean or wipe as necessary; store in covered container.	5–7
Lettuce, cucumber, cut onions, cut peppers, parsley	As above.	4–6
Cress, watercress	As above.	2

FOOD	HOW TO STORE	DAYS
Fresh fruit		
Cut oranges, grapefruit, lemons	In covered container.	3–4
Strawberries, red-currants, raspberries, peaches	As above.	1–3
Grapes, cherries, goose-berries, cut lemon	As above.	5–7
Rhubarb, cleaned	As above.	6–10
Eggs		
Fresh, in shell	In rack, pointed end down.	14
Yolks	In lidded plastic container.	2–3
Whites	As above.	3–4
Hardboiled, in shell	Uncovered.	up to 7
Fats		
Butter, margarine	In original wrapper, in special compartment of refrigerator.	14–21
Cooking fats	As above.	28
Milk, etc.		
Milk	In original container, closed.	3–4
Cream	As above.	2–4
Soured cream, butter-milk, yogurt	As above.	7
Milk sweets, custards	Lightly covered with foil or film.	2
Cheese		
Parmesan, in piece	In polythene film, foil, or airtight container.	21–28
Hard cheeses	As above.	7–14
Semi-hard cheeses	As above.	7–10
Soft (cream or curd) cheeses	As above.	5–7
Bread, rolls, etc.		
Any type of bread	In original waxed paper or polythene wrapper, or in foil.	7
Sandwiches	Wrap in foil or use tightly lidded plastic box; do not store if filling contains mayonnaise.	1–2
Leftovers		
Casseroles, pies, vegetables, cooked fruit	In original dish, tightly covered, or in plastic container.	2–4
Canned foods, opened	Leave in can but cover; fruits and fruit juices, which tend to alter slightly in flavour, are best put in another container.	As for freshly cooked foods

Standbys

Food	How to store	Days
Batter, uncooked	In covered jug or plastic container.	1–2
Pancakes, cooked	Interleaved with greaseproof paper and foil-wrapped.	7
Dry pastry mix	In screwtop jar or plastic container.	up to 14
Pastry, raw	Wrapped in foil.	2–3
Grated cheese	In lidded jar or plastic container.	up to 14
Stock, soup	In covered jug.	1–2

Larder and Food Cupboard Storage Times

FOOD	KEEPING QUALITIES, TIME	STORAGE COMMENTS
Flour, white	Up to 6 months	Once opened, transfer to container with close-fitting lid.
Wheatmeal	Up to 3 months	
Wholemeal	Up to 1 month	
Baking powder, bicarbonate of soda, cream of tartar	2–3 months	Dry storage essential; if opened, put in container with close-fitting lid.
Dried yeast	Up to 6 months	As above.
Cornflour, custard powder	Good keeping qualities	As above.
Pasta	As above	As above.
Rice, all types	As above	As above.
Sugar, loaf, caster, granulated	As above	Cool, dry storage; if opened, transfer as above.
Sugar, icing, brown	Limited life – tends to absorb moisture	Buy in small amounts as required.
Tea	Limited life – loses flavour if stored long	Buy in small amounts; store in airtight container in dry, cool place.
Instant and ground coffee in sealed can or jar	Up to 1 year	Cool, dry storage; once opened, re-seal securely; use quickly.
Coffee beans, loose ground coffee	Limited life; use immediately	Buy as required; use airtight container.
Instant low-fat skimmed milk	3 months	Cool, dry storage is vital; once opened, re-seal securely; use fairly quickly.
Breakfast cereals	Limited life	Buy in small quantities; cool, dry place. Fold inner wrapping down or transfer to an airtight container.
Dehydrated foods	Up to 1 year	Cool, dry place. If opened, fold packet down tightly and use within a week.

FOOD	KEEPING QUALITIES, TIME	STORAGE COMMENTS
Herbs, spices, seasonings	6 months	Cool, dry storage, in airtight container. Keep from light. Buy in small quantities.
Nuts, ground almonds, desiccated coconut	Limited life – depends on freshness when bought. Fat content goes rancid if kept too long.	Lidded container.
Dried fruits	2–3 months	Cool, dry storage.
Jams, etc.	Good keeping quality	Dry, cool, dark storage.
Honey, clear or thick	As above	Dry, cool storage. After about 1 year, appearance may alter, but still eatable.
Golden syrup, treacle	As above	As above.
Condensed milk	4–6 months	Safe even after some years, but caramelises and thickens. Once opened, harmless crust forms; cover can with foil lid and use within 1 month.
Evaporated milk	6–8 months	Safe even after some years, but darkens, thickens, and loses flavour. Once opened, treat as fresh milk.
Canned fruit	12 months	Cool, dry place.
Canned vegetables	2 years	Cool, dry place.
Canned fish in oil	Up to 5 years	Cool, dry place.
Canned fish in tomato sauce	Up to 1 year	Cool, dry place.
Canned meat	Up to 5 years	Cool dry place.
Canned ham	6 months	As above. Cans containing 2 lb. or more should be kept in refrigerator.
Pickles, sauces	Reasonably good keeping qualities	Cool, dry, dark place.
Chutneys	Limited life	As above.
Vinegars	At least up to 2 years	Cool, dry, dark place; strong light affects flavoured vinegar and produces a non-bacterial cloudiness. Re-seal after use; never return unused vinegar to bottle.
Oils (olive, corn)	Up to 18 months	Cool, dry place.

Some Menus to Cook Ahead

* Starred recipes are included in this book; refer to index for page numbers.

Chilled tomato juice
Cold glazed bacon*
Spiced peaches*
Jacket potatoes, Chicory salad
Lemon delight*

Smoked haddock ramekins*
Brown bread and butter
Lamb oysters*, Potato croquettes*,
    Minted peas
Melon and grapefruit jelly*

Grapefruit grill
Cod basque*, Creamed potatoes
Pineapple choco-crunch dessert*

Orange and walnut salad*
Bacon and mushroom pie
Lemon-dressed carrots
Blackcurrant cream*

Vegetable broth*   Bread sticks
Beef pies*, Green salad bowl
Fresh fruit, Lemon shorties*

Kipper pâté*   Melba toast
Roast duckling with grapefruit*
Broccoli, Sweetcorn, Duchesse potatoes*
Compote of apples with blackberries*

Chilled fruit juice
Chicken and lemon double crust pie*
Tomato coleslaw*
Pineapple and grape salad*

Taramasalata*
Burgundy beef*, Duchesse potatoes*,
    Coleslaw
Grape bavarois*

Mushrooms à la grecque*
Sage-and-bacon stuffed pork*
Fantail potatoes, Sliced green beans
Orange sorbet cups*

Ham and pineapple cocktail*
Osso buco*, Rice, Chicory salad
Crème marron*

Tomato jelly rings*
Rolled stuffed shoulder of lamb*
Roast potatoes, Cauliflower
Apple and orange Bristol*

Potted shrimps*
Flank of beef with horseradish*
Pan sauté potatoes with chives*,
    Mange-tout
Oranges à la turque*

Dressed chicory spears*
Arabian lamb*
Casseroled yellow rice*
Aubergine au gratin*
Lemon freeze*

Chilled cream of spinach soup*
Beef and pepper casserole*
Green salad
Raspberry cheese flan*

Tuna fish creams*
Pork chops in orange-pepper sauce*
Broccoli spears, Creamed potatoes
Pineapple meringue torte*

Marinaded mushrooms*
Glazed baked salmon garni*
French beans, Tomatoes, Asparagus
Strawberry Pavlova*

Courgettes à la grecque*
Beef Eldorado*
Peas, Sauté potatoes
Choc de menthe*

Avocado and melon cocktail*
Rolled stuffed breast of lamb*
Broccoli, Sauté potatoes
Choc au rhum*

Index